7/75

The Urban Neighborhood

Studies in Sociology

CONSULTING EDITOR
Charles H. Page
University of Massachusetts

RANDOM HOUSE   NEW YORK

The Urban Neighborhood:

A Sociological Perspective

Suzanne Keller

Princeton University

SECOND PRINTING

© Copyright, 1968, by Random House, Inc.
All rights reserved under International and Pan-American Copyright Conventions. Published in New York by Random House, Inc. and simultaneously in Toronto, Canada, by Random House of Canada Limited.
Library of Congress Catalog Card Number: 67–22331
Manufactured in the United States of America
Printed by Halliday Lithograph Corp., West Hanover, Mass.
Bound by H. Wolff Book Manufacturing, New York

This book is for
DR. JOSEF INFELD

Foreword

When dealing with human communities we must consider three major obligations. We have to understand *how* communities operate, *why* they operate as they do, and finally, to formulate our opinion about the way they *could best* operate.

I am of the opinion that we all make the grave mistake of concentrating too much on either the first aspect or on the third one: scientists tend to concentrate on the first and builders of societies, whether administrators or utopian thinkers, on the last. There is an imperative need for all of us to understand what happens, i.e. *why* communities operate the way they do and to look at this quite critically. This is necessary because there are many human communities that are structured in a way that gives free expression to their own wishes; in these instances it is natural that we respect these solutions highly. There are other human communities, however, that under the impact of the physical structure, the shells, and the networks that have been created all around them are not operating in the way they wish, but in the way they are forced to by the surroundings; in these cases we would be wrong to respect their solutions. We therefore must endeavor to understand the causes underlying these different "solutions" or outcomes, and then proceed to separate those which are satisfactory to man from those which are forced on him and which are therefore unsatisfactory.

It is for these reasons that the Athens Center of Ekistics tries to work on all three aspects of the problem; first we try to study what happens, then we try to explore the reasons and explain their effects, and, finally, we think that we have an obligation and should have the courage to propose solutions.

The Athens Center of Ekistics, in its effort to fulfill this purpose, has for the last six years been involved in the following major research projects: the "City of the Future," which endeavors to understand developing patterns and trends in the major settlements of the world today; the Growing Metropolitan Areas using the Athens metropolitan area as a model; and finally a number of smaller communities, which we have called human communities, in an effort to trace the impact of the human scale.

Related to the latter project is the subject of the neighborhood, which is the smallest unit operating in a city above the level of the family. This is not a clear notion though; it is sometimes clearer to speak about neighbors and neighboring than about a specific neighborhood. This important topic has become the subject of Dr. Keller's thorough study, which is expected to lead to a better understanding of what happens and also to proceed to its evaluation; it will, hopefully, also be a contribution to proposals concerning the future of urban neighboring and neighborhoods.

I am very glad that the first phases of this work, presented in this book under the title *The Urban Neighborhood: A Sociological Perspective*, were undertaken by Dr. Keller with the result that we now have a clearer basis for differentiating the general characteristics of neighboring and neighborhoods from the specific and geographically or culturally variable ones. Hopefully, this first synthesis will encourage comparable efforts in other research centers throughout the world and thus advance our knowledge of this important problem.

I do hope that this is only the beginning of an effort that will continue for a long time and that will cover as many cases as possible in order to help us understand these phenomena, their underlying causes, and our position toward them.

Athens, Greece   C. A. DOXIADIS
May 1967

Preface

This book grows out of research done under the auspices of the Athens Center of Ekistics where the author was a Fulbright Lecturer from 1963 to 1965 and then a regular employee of the organization (from 1965 to 1966 on a full-time basis; since 1966 on a part-time basis). Discussion and exchange of views with various ACE staff members proved stimulating and significant for the development of my thoughts on this topic and I wish to thank in particular the following persons: Dr. C. A. Doxiadis, President of Doxiadis Associates, Athens, Greece, for supporting—intellectually and financially— the research on which this book is based and for his critical advice and help; Mr. John G. Papaioannou, Director of Research of the Athens Center of Ekistics, for his interest and comments; Mrs. Doris Anagnostopoulou, architect planner at the ACE for a detailed, critical, and very helpful reading of the first draft of this book, which appears as Document RR–ACE, 68(105);

Mr. Panaghis Psomopoulos, Head of the International Programs Division of the ACE for a careful, provocative consideration of the original report as well as for the many hours during the preceding two years which he spent answering questions and helping me clarify my thoughts on the possible role of sociology in planning.

The final version of this book was prepared while the author was Visiting Professor of Sociology at Princeton University. My thanks go to Mrs. Mary W. Herman, Sociologist at the City of Philadelphia Community Renewal Program, and to Professor Arthur L. Stinchcombe, Department of Social Relations, Johns Hopkins University, for their useful suggestions; and to Leona Huberman and Charles H. Page for editorial help.

My gratitude also to Miss Alex Freme, ACE, Athens, and Miss Kathleen Kearney, Princeton University, for typing the manuscripts.

Princeton, N.J.   S. K.
December 1967

Contents

The Urban Neighborhood

Introduction

The aims of this book are practical—to synthesize
selected sociological evidence of relevance for physical planners in their work. Physical planners rarely have
the time to familiarize themselves with the various disciplines that have a bearing on the difficult task assigned
to them, not only because of the usual limitations of
time and energies, but also because interdisciplinary
thinking and communication are as yet in their infancy.
For example, it is obvious that sociology has something
to offer physical planning, but since sociology is oriented to its own special audience, its potential contribution to an applied field such as planning is often unreal-
ized. The two disciplines have much to give to each
other; however, their different emphasis, techniques,
and orientations prevent them from doing so easily and
successfully. Sociologists, with their penchant for ab-
stractions, for analysis, and for scrutiny of the present or
recent past, must first become sensitized to the styles

and aims of physical planners, with their focus on the practical, on diagnosis, and on change and developments in the future.

All this might simply be one more illustration of the price paid by professional overspecialization in the modern world were it not for the fact that both disciplines have a bearing on the organization of social life. When physical planners design houses and streets, community centers and transportation networks, neighborhood units and open spaces, they make many assumptions—most of them untested—about the ways in which people relate to one another, what needs exist in different groups, which needs have priority, and how social life may be influenced by physical design. Ideally, the planners should be able to draw on established sociological information on each of these points, but such knowledge is not, unfortunately, readily at hand.

Sociologists all too often state their generalizations in a form that ignores physical, spatial, and geographical factors and hence is too abstract for practical application. In part, this reflects their special predilections, but, in part, it is also a sign of insufficient exchanges between them and their potential collaborators in the framing of questions and the design of research. If there is as yet no organized body of sociological (as well as anthropological, historical, and psychological) evidence exclusively addressed to the problems of interest to physical planners, it is because such data presuppose some collaboration between these disciplines. Moreover, when physical planners often, and often rightly, criticize social scientists for being quick to condemn existing plans and proposals but not to assume responsibility for their formulation, they ignore the fact that they rarely specify their needs in a manner comprehensible to social scientists, even assuming that these would respond to their requests.

There is also the question of what, precisely, the social sciences can contribute to physical planning. The widely held conviction that they have a contribution to make is not, unfortunately, often matched by concrete illustrations of what it would comprise. There are vague references to the "link" between buildings and people, to the human factor, to man's basic needs, but only rarely are more concrete and explicit recommendations put forth.

In thus suggesting that the tools and knowledge of social science have a direct bearing on the physical planner's work, we are not claiming that these are as yet in a form to be of maximum use. We only insist that useful data are available, that more would be available if social scientists were more sensitive to what planners need, and that the present effort to assess and interpret such data may be considered one step in the building of a bridge between sociology and physical planning.

This immediately raises the problem of what might be the best point of attack. "Society," wrote Simone Weil, "itself is a force of nature, as blind as all other natural forces, and no less perilous to man unless he can achieve mastery over it." The modern metropolis, many would say, constitutes such a blind force that needs to be mastered. But while there is general agreement that something must be done, there is disagreement about specific targets and means. The philosophers would have men change their goals and values; the economists, their material standards of life; the psychologists, their passions and prejudices; and the city planners, their

physical environment. In truth, each of these suggestions has some value; not one can be ignored. In an
effort toward a more comprehensive approach properly
grounded in the facts and insights of two separate disciplines, we have chosen a problem of concern to both:
the place of local loyalties and attachments in metropolitan areas. What, we ask, is the sociological evidence for
or against the survival of neighboring and neighborhoods in the urban world? And how can physical planners achieve their objectives of (1) an equitable
distribution of facilities and services geared to meaningful local subunits and (2) stimulating local cooperation
among the residents?

As is the case with most unsolved social and moral
problems of our age, this issue of maintaining local self-
contained units has its partisans and its critics. There
are those who seek a solution to urban spiritual ills in
the construction of small, cohesive subunits that would
help recapture the local human scale; others advocate
the acceptance of the large, anonymous, urban aggregate as appropriate for modern living. The protagonists
argue that the creation of physically compact areas containing the basic human facilities and services while also
permitting close, informal, social ties among residents
would not only counteract alienation and instability but
also help distribute facilities and services more efficiently.[1] Their opponents argue that the longed-for fellowship and moral unity of the village and small town,
idealized in nostalgic recall, was not primarily an expression of the small scale of these settlements. It was an
expression of an overlap and intertwining of a number
of economic, social, and moral forces without which the
small scale would hardly have achieved its ostensible

effects. The small town and cohesive village that "lives on in the imaginations of moralists, poets, old men, and city planners"[2] was a constellation of many different forces of which size and scale were only the most visible indicators. To select that one dimension out of context and apply it under changed conditions is bound to prove a disappointment. The human scale, as important in the metropolis as in the village, may no longer, in a world of speed and space, coincide with the local scale.

Catherine Bauer and C. A. Doxiadis express the two poles of the argument vividly. Bauer summarizes the opposition to the neighborhood principle as "reactionary in effect and sentimental in concept," ignoring the trends in modern society "away from localized 'ingroups' and small parochial communities"—as "an escape, a rationalization of the real problems we fear to face."[3] Doxiadis, on the other hand, pleads for the "human dimensions" in the world's cities, of which the neighborhood provides one measure: ". . . the community of the neighborhood—the local community— . . . was a natural community. We see no reason why it should be taken away from man. Additional ties are, of course, necessary, but why should they deprive man of the natural local ties?"[4]

How natural are these ties? Can we do without them? Will the children of tomorrow miss the local neighborhood any more than we miss the villages of our grandparents? To help clarify this issue, we clearly need more information on the habits, manners, and morals of individuals and groups in villages and cities, in the old central districts and the newer suburbs, in settlements inhabited by people ever on the move and in those of settled, stable populations. "What sorts of people tend to move about freely and for what purposes? Who are the people who cling to a district whether it has advantages or not? And if we build neighborhoods, how self-contained should they be? How isolated? Is the size of 1000–1500 households not wrong—too small for urban variety and too large for genuine neighboring?" [5] We still know very little about how people themselves divide a city, what they get out of local areas, and the importance they attach to neighborhoods. "We have no evidence," according to Doxiadis, "that the community of the district, the community of the neighborhood, is not required today, and yet we destroy it." [6]

At this point, both among protagonists and opponents of the neighborhood ideal, the plea ultimately is for more knowledge, for more precise answers so that future policy may be more soundly based. Which is closer to the truth for what sorts of people, "to love thy neighbor as thyself" or that "good fences make good neighbors"?

Intimate, small-scale units that promise to be both equitable and efficient have a powerful appeal in this century of the common man. However, two challenges confront this view. One is essentially philosophical in nature—postulating a new urban man and considering the current sweep toward megalopolis as a force that not only transcends but also will eventually extinguish the village ethos inspiring the neighborhood idea. The other rests on information about characteristic desires and activities of urbanites, as revealed in objective inquiries, that fail to coincide with those assumed by the neighborhood unit concept. The first challenge is more properly the subject of a moral discourse and beyond the scope of this book. The second is well within our purview and constitutes, in fact, one of our main objectives. In the pages to follow, the evidence on neighbor relations and neighborhood identity and attachment will be examined to help answer questions about the utility of neighborhood units in the modern urban complexes of our time.

This study does not claim to be an exhaustive survey of sociological studies nor to touch on all the relevant issues in this highly controversial field. It only hopes to open the way for reducing the gap between analytic social science and practical planning. The book is divided into four parts. Chapter 1 dissects the analytical components of the terms "neighborhood" and "neighboring" that colloquial usage tends to ignore or obscure; Chapter 2 summarizes a range of selected sociological evidence on kinds and amounts of neighboring, patterns of neighboring, and the meaning of neighborhoods; and Chapters 3 and 4 discuss the implications of the findings for physical planners.

SOME METHODOLOGICAL PROBLEMS ■

CONCEPTUAL AMBIGUITY ■

Before turning to the substance of this study, we shall briefly consider the conceptual and methodological difficulties confronting the investigator engaged in synthesizing existing information for planning purposes. The first problem is that of varied and often inconsistent definitions of terms and concepts.

Both in physical planning and in sociology, the term "neighborhood" has been widely, variously, and often inconsistently used. At times it seems to refer to an area having certain physical properties, at times to a set of human activities and relationships, and then again to an area in which such activities or relationships may, but need not, occur. C. H. Cooley, the American social theorist, considered the neighborhood, along with the family and playmates, to be a primary group, and many physical planners similarly confound the spatial and social dimensions of neighboring.[7] Before one can properly assess the current state of knowledge on neighborhoods in modern urban settings, therefore, one must first clarify the various conceptions and assumptions contained within that ambiguous term.

The existing confusion is the result of at least three factors:

1. Conceptual ambiguity, particularly the failure to distinguish between three essential, yet separate, elements—that of the neighbor as a special role and relationship, that of neighboring as a more broadly defined set of activities and relations, and that of the neighborhood as a delimited area in which neighboring and activities involving neighbors may occur.

2. Contradictory research evidence based on ambiguous assumptions and instruments. We are told, for example, that there is little neighborhood spirit in community X because few informants are friends with their neighbors. But even the most impeccable research findings regarding friendly ties among neighbors cannot convey an accurate picture of *neighborly* ties among neighbors if these two are, as appears to be the case, distinct relationships. If most neighborly relations are, in fact, not relations of friendship, then to ask only about those that are causes us to miss the large majority that are not. Unless the phe-

nomenon to be investigated is explicitly defined, it is virtually impossible to distinguish the essential from the accidental elements and so to discover genuine rather than spurious empirical variations in neighboring activities and relationships. In our previous example, ignoring the distinction between friend and neighbor may lead to unwarranted inferences about the alienation of modern urban man and to unwarranted idealization of the friendly neighbors in small towns and peasant villages. The failure of planners to re-create such "friendly" neighborhoods in the modern metropolis may thus be due less to any professional shortcomings than to their being ill-advised as to the conditions making for friendship and for neighborliness in village and city.

3. The problem of rapid social change upsetting the traditional balance between neighbors, neighboring, and neighborhoods and leaving in its wake a residue of disconnected fragments of such neighborhoods. As the relatively compact and easily identifiable subareas of small towns and stable cities disintegrated under the impact of the industrial-urban tidal wave, there often remained only broken bits of such neighborhoods or planners' idealized images of them. Studies of these neighborhood fragments then show them to be areas of variable and vague boundaries and of unrelated activities and relationships. In place of the more or less unified social and spatial entities of the past we observe the sprawling, seemingly formless, rapidly changing aggregates within which the mobile urban multitude is forging the personal and social relations of its time. This poses great difficulties to the investigator of neighborhood cohesion. Even the most distinctive "natural areas" of cities (those with homogeneous populations, a

historic identity, strong social traditions, and considerable stability) cannot escape the pressure toward ceaseless and rapid movement and heterogeneity that transforms these neighborhoods into hybrid creatures suspended between past and future. In the absence of clearly defined concepts it is not possible to form correct impressions of these events, nor to record and measure them precisely.

To avoid these pitfalls, this study, therefore, proposes three important conceptual distinctions. There is, first, the neighbor as a special role implying a particular kind of social attitude toward others to be distinguished from the role of friend and of relative with which it may at times merge, as when relatives may be living next door or when neighbors become friends. Second, there are various activities associated with this role ranging from highly formalized and regular neighborly rituals to sporadic, informal, and casual contacts. Third, there is the area itself—the neighborhood—where neighbors reside and in which neighboring takes place. This may be a clearly demarcated spatial unit with definite boundaries and long-established traditions or a fluid, vaguely defined subpart of a town or city whose boundaries are only vaguely apparent and differently perceived by its inhabitants.

OPERATIONAL INADEQUACIES ■

Our understanding of phenomena depends on the nature and interpretation of available evidence. Interpretation means making logically connected inferences based on observed data whose quality and utility is in turn dependent on the sources of information consulted and the techniques used to obtain it. Two of the main

sources of information on neighboring and neighborhoods are knowledgeable or representative samples of
informants and collected (tabulated or mapped) statis-
tics. The techniques used to tap these sources have included participant observation and the informal recording of neighborhood life in local communities, direct
questioning of respondents in formal interview settings
as in sample surveys, and the inferring of neighboring
activities and relationships from specially computed
rates of collective characteristics and behavior.

Most investigators have been interested in one of two
questions: (1) How much neighboring occurs in a
given area or among a given group? (2) Do neighborhoods function as distinct spatial entities within larger
communities? The answers depend on consistent opera-
tional definitions and reliable research instruments.
And, as we shall see, the problems of locating boundaries, of sampling, and of interviewing are reflected in
the evidence accumulated.

BOUNDARIES ▪

The attempt to locate neighborhoods by means of
agreed-upon boundaries founders on the fact that the
most clear-cut physical and symbolic boundaries go
hand in hand with clear-cut neighborhoods of which
these boundaries are only indicators. Where neither
tradition nor relative isolation helps forge such boundaries, they cannot, apparently, be drawn with any accu-
racy.

Thus Riemer points to the danger of studying a delimited and contiguous "patch of the urban fabric and
recording activities sustained in such areas" since,
thereby, important social activities that do not take

place in these areas remain hidden and are treated as nonexistent.[8]

SAMPLING ■

Most studies of neighborhood activities and the use of local facilities are based on interviews with housewives, who supposedly engage in more neighboring and are more involved with local neighborhood activities. This limitation is not, however, always kept in mind when generalizing from the answers supplied by them to "families" or "the working class" or the "urban dweller." Even if these housewives are asked about their husbands' or their children's neighboring activities, they may not be able to supply the correct information. Moreover, a certain bias is bound to be introduced when interviews are concentrated on functioning households, excluding the more transient residents, the unmarried, the highly mobile, and others who may not be available for home interviews.

QUESTIONNAIRE DESIGN ■

It is well known that the nature of the questions asked may determine the answers given. Frequently, a problem may have little saliency for individuals and yet elicit dutiful responses to direct questions. In a West Philadelphia study, for example, when people were asked what they considered to be the biggest problem in the area, one-third could think of none. These same respondents, however, when asked specific questions about particular problems involving housing, noise, crime, unemployment, and so on, indicated concern about these problems.[9] Here, as in the next question, some forcing of answers is probably unavoidable by the very structure of the questions. When urban residents in San Juan are asked to indicate their three best friends among their neighbors, what do their positive answers really mean? The question not only does not reveal what each respondent has in mind when he thinks of his "best" friend, but also presupposes that there will be such friendships among neighbors. Similarly, if housewives are asked whether their husband's "three closest recreational friends" are the same as their own, will any of them say that they or their husbands have no close friends, or only one, or will they give the answers they feel are expected of them? The last two questions, drawn from one of the more sophisticated studies in this field,[10] well illustrate the difficulty of designing proper questions. The same holds true for other aspects of the study design such as sampling, interviewing, index formation, and scale construction—all useful if carefully designed, pretested, and applied but of dubious value if they are not.

Of the hundreds of studies consulted for this book not one is sufficiently comprehensive in scope, design, or locale to serve as an absolutely reliable source of data or model of procedure. Most studies are confined to small areas of local communities or to limited samples and emphasize only a few of the relevant dimensions of this complex subject of neighboring. We have already indicated that there is considerable ambiguity in the terms themselves, and this conceptual confusion is often matched by confusing research evidence based on arbitrary definition of terms, inadequate samples, and unreliable instruments. Thus, by confounding the distinction between neighbor and friend, studies often report less neighboring in cities than would be shown to exist were other definitions of neighboring used. Nor is the meaning of replies always fully explored. If people are asked whether they like their neighborhood, they usually say yes; but without knowing where they draw the boundary lines or which aspect of the neighborhood they may be thinking of (the people near them, the shops and cinemas, the access to the center, or the reputation of the area as a smart place), it is virtually impossible to make sense of their answers and thereby to accumulate valid and reliable knowledge.

If we do not as yet have scientifically valid knowledge of the formation and functioning of neighborhoods, it is probably due to the conceptual difficulties involved in designing studies to yield such knowledge. To help develop such designs, it is necessary to collect and classify the existing evidence based on personal impressions and fragments of existing studies. By thus piecing together, as this book tries to do, the many varied bits of evidence gathered in as many varied ways, a fairly consistent set of relevant dimensions may be specified. This method, tedious, time-consuming, and cumbersome though it be, is useful as a preliminary step in helping to guide more systematic research efforts in the future.

In truth, it is astonishing that these hundreds of studies of respondents in different contexts answering, perhaps unreliably, lists of unsystematic questions have managed to yield as consistent findings as they do regarding, for example, rural and urban differences in neighboring and the role of physical design in neighboring. Of course, their consistency and agreement are partly a function of the sort of questions one has in mind since facts rarely tell their own story. However, armed with a few concepts, primitive and preliminary though they be, provided by the exploration of existing data, we, at least, can make a reasonable beginning of our study of neighbors and neighboring. The available data give us a reasonable summation of what we know and do not know about the role of neighboring and neighborhoods in the cities and towns of our era. It is with these qualifications that we proceed with the discussion.

1 Neighbors and Neighboring

A careful look at the patterns of association among different groups and settings suggests that neighboring is neither natural nor inevitable. Before individuals are able to develop sustained and meaningful relationships with neighbors, they must first have a clear idea of what a neighbor is expected to be and to do. And if these neighborly relations are to be predictable and orderly to some degree, they must be rooted in a shared fund of ideas and beliefs. Barring this, neighbor relations will either fail to be established or, if established, they will be unreliable and ineffectual.

THE NEIGHBOR ROLE ■

We may, using technical sociological language, refer to the crystallized aspects of neighborly relations within a group or population as the "neighbor role." If a group has participated in a common environment for some, as yet undetermined, period of time, it will usually have developed some shared expectations as to the demands of this role. These demands, as the following example illustrates, are not uniform. The neighbor role may be clearly defined but involve minimal interpersonal contacts, or it may be loosely defined and yet imply close and continual interpersonal exchanges.

Let us consider the example of a working class district, X, where people have strong and solid neighboring traditions demanding that neighbors respond unhesitatingly to requests for tools, money, food, or advice and that, in turn, people feel free to ask their neighbors for such assistance. Any individual, therefore, in the course of his own life will be both borrower and lender. The role is not ambiguous, and there is agreement about its specifications and demands.

Let us consider as a second example another working class district, Y, where there are equally strong expectations about what neighbors should and should not do, may or may not ask and give. But this time the content of the expected relation is quite different. Beyond polite greetings, people are expected to keep to themselves, to mind their own business, to stay out of other people's affairs, and neither to give nor to ask for favors. Furthermore, it is expected that everyone will do his share in maintaining physical and social standards by not being too noisy, keeping streets and common facilities clean and proper, and observing the rules of social conduct.

The difference in the two conceptions lies in the content of what is expected of good neighbors, not in the strictness or strength of the definition. How good a neighbor one is depends on the general importance assigned to the role; what a good neighbor should do depends, as we shall see, on specific values and preferences. In both examples, the particular version of what a neighbor is or should be is firmly established and seems right and proper to the members. So long as each group keeps to itself, things will proceed more or less smoothly.

Trouble is bound to arise, however, if an individual from district Y were to find himself living in district X. He would then probably consider his neighbors as impossibly intrusive, gossipy, and interfering. They, in turn, will most likely find him aloof, snobbish, selfish, and unfriendly. These judgments are quite consistent in light of the different conceptions of neighbors held by each. If the individual from Y decides to continue to live there, some effort will have to be made by one or both sides to change their behavior and along with it the conception on which this behavior is based. If they fail to do so, the individual from Y will feel unhappy in his new environment and the people in X will consider him an undesirable neighbor.

These examples are instructive for our purposes because they suggest that the type of neighboring to be found in an area will generally reflect the concepts prevailing there of what a good neighbor is expected to be or to do. A good neighbor is not necessarily a friendly or a nice person but one who conforms to the standards of the neighbor role common consent acknowledges. The frictions that may arise between groups or individuals holding different conceptions of this role may be due to these, often intangible, differences rather than to their aggressive or pugnacious natures, or to particular physical arrangements of houses and gossip squares. External physical and social arrangements are thus sustained by an unseen inner core of belief and expectations defining these. In view of cultural and historic variety, no single definition of neighbor is universally accepted, and planners of the human environment must, therefore, try to determine at the outset how the neighbor role is defined in order to assess its local significance in any particular setting.

However, while there is no single comprehensive or universally shared definition of neighbor, several essential elements appear to lie at the heart of the concept.

THE NEIGHBOR AS A STRANGER ■

If, as in some simple villages, neighbors are also clan and blood relations, then the concept of neighbor cannot arise. It arises precisely because the neighbor is the proximate stranger, defending interests that are partly his alone and partly those he shares with other neighbors. From the start this burdens the relation with ambiguity as regards the limits of intimacy and the depth of mutual involvement. In most tribal and peasant villages this presents no real problem, for though the neighbor may be considered a stranger in the sense of not being a blood or affinal relative, he is, nonetheless, a familiar figure whose antecedents are as well known as his current habits. In cities, however, the neighbor may actually be a total stranger, one whose ancestors and habits are unknown and whose true personality must be pieced together from fragments revealed only in the course of time.

THE NEIGHBOR AS SPATIALLY BUT NOT NECESSARILY SPIRITUALLY CLOSE ▪

Nearness and distance, though spatial concepts, depend on more than space. Friends may live far apart and yet remain in spiritual communion. Neighbors may be worlds apart even though they live next door. This tension between physical proximity and spiritual uncertainty adds to the ambivalence of the relationship as individuals are ever moved by twin impulses—to look at neighbors subjectively as they would at themselves or to look at them objectively as they would at strangers. Although this may be a problem anywhere, it is more crucial in small communities where escape from difficult or intolerable neighbors is not readily possible. Not surprisingly, then, it is in these communities that definitions of the neighbor role and the rules regulating conduct among neighbors are most clear-cut, rigid, proscribed, and formalized. To minimize conflict and to preserve some privacy under conditions of physical proximity it is necessary to maintain some psychological distance even in the most intimate relationships. This is even more necessary in relationships where, as among neighbors, the partners are both near and distant, joined and yet separate.

The consensus as to what the neighbor role is and the degree of formality of the role vary with the importance of services rendered by neighbors to one another. Where the need for these services is great and the neighbor's contribution is thus indispensable and irreplaceable, the role is rigidly defined and firmly anchored in local customs and habits. This is likely to be the case in rural villages, small towns, and special cultural enclaves in large cities; that is, wherever people are thrown back upon their own limited resources but can muster up enough collective spirit to mobilize these for emergencies. Excluded are all groups who, either because of excessive individualism or an extreme passivity and submissiveness to fate, are unable to join forces for the sake of the common good. Hopelessness and fatalism in the face of desperate poverty, or brutal authority, or both may lead to that peculiar constriction of social ties characteristic of some backward villages or abandoned wastelands of cities. Under such conditions the concept of neighbor, not to speak of the good neighbor, is non-existent.

THE DISTINCTION BETWEEN NEIGHBOR, FRIEND, AND KIN ■

The neighbor is thus neither a relative nor a friend because the first is a prescribed relationship, which one must acknowledge though one need not cherish it, and the second is a chosen one. You do not lose the relative by ignoring him, but you cannot keep the friend if you do. The neighbor, like the relative, is somehow an objectively given, inescapable presence in one's life space. However, some choice exists here, too, as to what one decides to make of this relationship, how one feels about it and gets along in it, which resembles the selectivity characterizing friendships. Neighbors differ from both relatives and friends, however, in that physical distance does not destroy these relationships whereas a neighbor, by definition, ceases to exist as a neighbor once spatial distance intervenes. Thus, the neighbor differs from the friend in the following ways:

1. Physical proximity is significant for the creation and maintenance of the relationship. Friends may be made anywhere—where one lives, plays, or works. Neighbors are by definition those who reside next to or near one. The degree or extent of nearness varies, but it is always an element in the relationship.

2. The neighbor relation is usually, at least, in part collectively defined and has wider social implications than does friendship, which is generally a private and personal affair. Unlike neighbor relations, neither the formation nor the termination of a friendship has direct and unmistakable collective consequences except under very special conditions. But the discontinuance of neighbor relations, especially where these relations are an essential part of social life, has a direct collective impact.

3. The degree of personal intimacy and total personal involvement of the partners differ. The very basis of friendship is a close reciprocity rooted in mutual trust, affection, and respect. A neighborly relation, on the other hand, is more limited and less intimate.

The role of neighbor, no matter how defined, is a supplement to other roles involving men in sustained bonds of dependency, each contributing some unique element. The neighbor replaces—but does not displace—the distant friend or relative by performing tasks that the friend or relative is unable to perform. But to be a good neighbor is not at all the same as to be a good friend. If you become good friends with your neighbor, the friendship relation usurps the neighbor relation. The degree to which individuals transform neighbor relations into kinship or friendship relations probably varies by group and setting, but once the neighbor relation is so transformed, it has ceased to exist solely as a neighbor relation.

The essential differences between neighbors, kin, and friends have been noted repeatedly. Good neighbors, it has been said, are friendly but not friends. It is not uncommon to hear, "If I wanted to borrow I might go to a neighbor, but if I were in real trouble, I would go to friends." You lose a friend by failing him; you lose a neighbor by moving away; you never lose a relative except through death.

Thus, the role of neighbor fits into a network of social roles and its explicitness depends on the nature of the social organization, including the density of settlements, the distance between dwelling units, the economic well-being of the inhabitants, the degree of cooperation demanded or permitted among residents, and the general trust placed by individuals in nonrelatives. Since neither the needs of residents nor the conditions giving rise to these needs are universal or uniform, we find considerable variations among settlements in (1) the distinctiveness of the neighbor role, (2) its saliency relative to other roles, (3) the formality and rigidity of its definition, and (4) the degree of consensus as to the rights and duties associated with it.

EVIDENCE ON THE ROLE OF NEIGHBOR ■

Since most studies do not clearly distinguish between the neighbor role and neighboring activities, evidence on the components of the neighbor role in different cultural and social settings is sparse. An exception is provided by a study of elderly East London residents who had lived in their district for many years and whose lives were intertwined with those of the other residents by intensive and durable ties of work, family, schooling, and clubs.[1] The author made special efforts to tap neighbor relations as distinct from other types, but a number of difficulties stood in his way. First, he found that many friends and neighbors were also relatives, and this intertwining of relationships made it virtually impossible to disentangle them for purposes of discussion. Then there was the implicit tendency to redefine neighbors that had become friends. "Often a neighbour with whom there was a close relationship was no longer thought to be a neighbour but a friend. Thus a question about neighbours was interpreted by many people to apply only to those non-relatives living around them who were not friends." He finally defined the term "neighbor" operationally to mean any "unrelated person living in the same street or block, with whom there was a customary or prearranged contact at least once a month on the average." [2] The term "friend" was defined as an unrelated person not living in the same street or block with whom some customary prearranged contact was arranged once a month. By these definitions 66 percent of the respondents had regular contacts with unrelated persons. Few of them had such contacts as often as once or twice a week, however, whereas most saw relatives every day or nearly every day.

Here, as elsewhere, neighbor relations were normatively defined, but norm and fact did not always coincide. Old people prided themselves on the fact that they kept to themselves, very seldom saw anything of their neighbors, and neither visited nor were visited by them. At the same time, however, they definitely relied on neighbors for help in fetching relatives or doctors when illness struck, for borrowing utensils or food on occasion, and for acting as intermediaries between them and outsiders such as bill collectors or callers. Nevertheless, they distinguished between neighbors in their roles as providers of information about other residents and as go-betweens with other families, and neighbors as intimate participants in one's life. Definite boundaries were drawn beyond which neighbors should not venture if they hoped to maintain civil relationships among themselves. Contacts with neighbors were recognized as fleeting, impermanent, and not intimate, based on courtesy and convenience rather than on love and deep personal involvement. Their "lives were vaguely bound up with yours because they shared the same scene, the same kind of houses, the same political representatives, and the same shortages." [3] They were part of a familiar environment. This suggests that personal relations among neighbors are not essential for attachment to them or to an area, that, in fact, the personal bonds are indirect by-products of larger impersonal forces shaped by tradition, current styles of life, and a common destiny.

There seems to be a general tendency among urban residents to keep neighbor relations delimited and to handle neighbors with care. One London housewife, for example, knew many of her female neighbors but, nevertheless, "took it for granted that a friendly relationship with a neighbor would end if the woman went away." [4] For a majority of residents on two British housing estates the "main issue for most people was . . . the importance of maintaining the distinction between a friend and an acquaintance, and of keeping neighbourly relations within the bounds of acquaintanceship." [5] The notion of the neighbor as somehow alien who must help but not intrude is a fairly general one.[6]

Essentially, the neighbor is the helper in times of need who is expected to step in when other resources fail. These needs range from minor routine problems to major crises, and the help requested may be material or spiritual. Moreover, the help asked for and given is not unlimited but carefully, though often informally, prescribed. It is called forth in situations that spell danger to a group or community as in times of natural disasters and unforeseen calamities, or that routinely afflict any and everyone so that the help you give today you may ask for tomorrow.

THE CONCEPT OF NEIGHBORING ■

Neighboring refers to the activities engaged in by neighbors *as neighbors* and the relationships these engender among them. Though role-determined to some extent, these activities are broader and less crystallized, consisting of organized as well as random elements. Groups vary as to the kinds and amounts of neighboring in which their members engage, and individuals vary as to which of several dimensions—priority, intensity, frequency, and occasion—they emphasize. As we shall see, patterns of neighboring reflect the character of the individuals engaging in it as well as the dynamics of their ways of life.

Studies have generally been concerned about how much neighboring exists in a given area or group without, however, separately assessing its several dimensions. People may be asked to indicate whom they see, know, talk to, visit, or help, at which times and for what reasons, the questions varying from simple, unstructured ones eliciting their "free" associations to highly structured ones, demanding fairly categorical replies that may be scaled.[7] Inadequate conceptualization marks many of these studies: one investigator asks only about neighborly visits, another mainly about the exchange of help during emergencies, and a third about friendships. The absence of a systematic framework results in uneven, piecemeal information that fails to add up to a balanced, comprehensive account.

Neighboring activities and relationships thus include a predictable core element based on the neighbor role and additional nonpredictable elements reflecting the social and personal context in which neighboring typically takes place. The second aspect cannot be deduced from a knowledge of the role but must be observed and assessed from case to case. A number of different patterns may develop out of varied combinations of these dimensions, and people may agree on the essentials of the neighbor role without exhibiting identical patterns of neighboring. In the section that follows the evidence for neighboring activities and neighboring relationships will be discussed separately.

NEIGHBORING ACTIVITIES ■

CONTENT ■

The neighbor is expected to help in times of need, ranging from routine household requests for items of food or from help with a child to cyclical help with the harvest or housebuilding or in major crises such as floods, fires, and epidemics. Exchanging tools, informal visiting, and asking advice are among the more frequently mentioned activities.[8]

Although the exchange of help in crisis seems to be universally associated with neighboring and is one of its key justifications, there are considerable variations by culture, group, and class as to what is considered a crisis or need. For example, one cross-cultural study of English and American residents on two housing estates showed that the English disapproved of borrowing food or household items but considered the exchange of garden tools natural and normal. For the Americans, on the other hand, who did the bulk of their shopping by car, borrowing food was included in their conception of good neighboring.[9] Among the residents of a German industrial suburb neighboring also involved borrowing and lending, but with many constraints reflecting a concern with one's reputation. Thus, one could freely borrow an iron (as this may on occasion fail to work) but not a pot for cooking since a good household is expected to have one.[10] Similar variations as to what is considered respectable were found in two British working class communities. In the more traditional one having neighbors in to gossip was frowned upon; in the new housing estate such disapproval extended to dropping in on neighbors unexpectedly, borrowing without prompt return or repayment, and prying into neighbors' affairs. Privacy and restraint were highly valued as well.[11] In German rural villages in the past recreational activities, such as card playing, story telling, or drinking, were associated with neighborly cooperation and were especially common after help with the harvest or canning of food.[12]

OCCASIONS FOR NEIGHBORING ■

Personal crises, collective emergencies, and big collective events, such as marriages and funerals, constitute the chief occasions for neighboring. In a North German industrial suburb, working class tenants in four-to-five-story apartment houses considered participation in death a universal obligation, help in sickness more or less universal, but joining in marriage or religious festivities more properly matters for the particular families involved.[13] The two most commonly cited occasions for neighborly help among a low income Baltimore sample involved sickness in the family or some problem with the children.[14] In Liverpool neighbors were turned to for minor emergencies related to the household, help with shopping, or posting a letter as well as during dramatic moments of confinement or bereavement. The latter reveals the existence of what has been called "latent" neighborliness.[15]

In more traditional rural settings one often notes great neighborly interdependence on such occasions as the harvest, housebuilding, or planting or during emergencies such as fires. All aspects of death involve neighborly help—from the funeral to the wake—as do marriage, baptism, and communion. All this tends to change as self-interest and egotism enter into neighbor relations. The more urban the settlements, the more pronounced these trends.[16]

LOCALE ▪

The places where neighbors exchange tools, ideas, or advice vary from home to front door to the street. Some groups do not permit neighbors into their houses; others see them only there. Some districts have traditions of neighboring resting on regular encounters in the local pub, dance hall, shop, or church, whereas in other districts neighboring consists of casual meetings on the street while going on errands or before entering one's own front door. Social class considerations seem to play a role in this. In working class districts people do not usually invite nonrelatives into their homes but meet them on the street, at work, or at the pub, all of these being nearby.[17]

NEIGHBORING RELATIONSHIPS ▪

The activities and occasions for neighboring give rise to a number of more or less strong bonds or links among neighbors. These links among variously connected individuals lend an area a characteristic web of social relationships. Short of being totally isolated from social and emotional contact with others, a state reserved, according to Aristotle, for beasts or for gods, most individuals maintain some ties with at least one of the following— relatives, neighbors, or friends. Limited time, energy, resources, and needs as well as variations in traditional standards and personal inclination account for the differential saliency of these three types of social bonds. Thus, not only the role of what a neighbor is and should do varies from group to group, but also its relative priority. Evidence suggests that if people are totally taken up with relatives, they will not cultivate ties with friends or neighbors. Neighbors become important when relatives are not available or where people lack the skills or opportunities to make friends.

PRIORITY OF NEIGHBORS ■

The importance attached to an occasion determines whether one will consult a neighbor or a relative. On one British working class estate people said that if they had to borrow bread, they would turn to a neighbor, but if there were some more serious matters such as illness, they would turn to a relative.[18] Another sample of British workers likewise indicated that they would rely on relatives rather than friends or neighbors in times of emergency, but in this instance the relatives referred to daughters actually living at the same address. These illustrations reflect a general tendency among working class families to confine their social relations to family, only occasionally to neighbors, less frequently to kinsmen, and only rarely to friends.[19] As these families become more self-reliant and independent of group influences in matters pertaining to child rearing, style of life, and interests, they rely even less on neighbors. This is true even for rural villages only recently touched by industrialization and improved material standards of life.[20] The sanctions available to a group may determine the importance attached to maintaining good relations with it. In Tokyo, for example, where etiquette may compel that formal attention be paid to one's neighbors, neighbors may, nevertheless, have less priority than do business acquaintances or fellow employees whose sanctions are greater than those available to neighbors.[21]

In general, people divide their time between friends, neighbors, and relatives according to some formal or informal order of priorities. Traditional, stable, settled communities probably rely more on relatives, but as these tend also to be neighbors, their respective influence cannot be ascertained. There does seem to be a tendency for the importance of friends to increase as the environment becomes more urban and heterogeneous, but, while the range of kin obligations also narrows, ties to family and kin decline less sharply than do those to neighbors.[22]

The priority of neighboring relationships is in part status-determined. Thus, while people generally prefer to be self-sufficient and not to have to borrow at all, if they must borrow, they prefer to do so from status equals.[23] Perhaps for this reason people may actually deny the extent of their neighboring so as to create an impression of independence and self-reliance. One group of elderly residents "were apt to deny indignantly that they ever visited their neighbors, even where, in practice, such visiting was common and self-evident." [24]

In addition, neighbor relations oscillate between openness and reserve and between intimacy and distance, and both too great intimacy and too great controversy are to be avoided. Hence, the contents of a proper conversation with neighbors may involve the weather, household matters, and children but not politics or job matters.[25]

In urban areas neighboring is apparently more elastic than in rural areas, ranging from casualness during periods of quiet routine to intense activity during emergencies. Accordingly, the formality, frequency, and range of such relationships are more difficult to assess for urbanites.

FORMALITY OF RULES GOVERNING NEIGHBOR RELATIONS ■

In the past it was not uncommon to have neighbor obligations embodied in formal rules and regulations. In the German villages studied by Wurzbacher bridge and road building were in the hands of formal collective organizations of neighbors, whereas other activities were informally controlled by the inhabitants. Each member of a particular district was obligated to respond to a call for help on any occasion but especially during harvests and housebuilding as well as in times of collective crises.[26]

Max Weber referred to the typically recurring exception as a cause of the institutionalization and formalization of neighbor relations into protective, work, or recreational associations.[27] All the activities that require mutual aid and that affect communal or individual well-being but are not provided for by existing institutions become the responsibility of local neighborhood groups. Under these conditions the responsibilities neighbors owe to each other are left neither to chance nor to individual inclination; they are embodied in an unwritten law, reflecting a basic, perhaps unconscious, consensus, which regulates the conduct of neighbors, the feelings of trust they should express toward one another, and the debts that they owe and how and when to repay them. The neighbor relation thus becomes a contractual relation differing only in that no fixed time of repayment is usually specified, the contract being fulfilled as the need arises.[28]

Another instance of explicit rules governing neighbor relations concerns highly urbanized Tokyo where, according to Dore, the etiquette of neighbor relations is so highly formalized as to constitute a "social fact" in Durkheim's sense. "It is something which is conceived as an objectively established body of rules, subject to local variation and capable of being learned and taught, not simply as 'natural' ways of behaving which can safely be left to the spontaneous promptings of the individual heart to take care of." [29] These rules, embodied in an institution known as the five-man-group system or the five-household-group system of collective responsibility, functioned in both towns and villages where they helped "keep sweet" those highly significant neighbor relations on which economic cooperation depended. And now, even the informal units of neighboring, the *tonari-gumi*, are formally part of the collective organization of urban wards. They include only ten-to-twenty households, but informal neighbor relations are carried on with no more than three-to-four neighbors living in houses on either side and opposite to one's own. These neighbors express complete trust in each other, lend and borrow freely, and act as guardians of each other's houses, health, and reputations. Today such intimate ties are naturally confined only to those who stay at home all day—housewives and local shopkeepers. Such formal rules did much to help rural Japanese migrants adjust to the bewildering world of the city. Not many cities in other parts of the world help their newcomers in this way, although all might benefit from the adoption of some such scheme.

FREQUENCY OF NEIGHBORLY CONTACTS ■

Many studies do not provide information about how frequently neighbors are in contact. This may be indirect proof of the significance of neighboring wherever it is not subject to traditional or formal controls and where individuals regulate these contacts on their own. At the same time it is difficult to obtain precise figures simply because neighbors often see each other involuntarily in the course of other routine activities. Sparse though the existing information is, it suggests quite a range of frequencies among different groups from daily to weekly to monthly encounters.[30]

EXTENT OF NEIGHBORLY CONTACTS ■

Data are also sparse for the range of contacts. Most people seem to know several others in the areas in which they live, but this depends, in addition to personal and group standards, on how long they have lived there and on how residentially stable the area is. Probably all residents have contacts with some of their neighbors, but the range is wide—from two-thirds who knew the Christian names of at least one of their neighbors on a working class housing estate to one-half who "knew" another tenant in their apartment house located in a North German industrial suburb.[31] It is rare to be close to many neighbors—and only minorities are. Even where neighbor relations are formally prescribed, as in Tokyo, about one-half of those interviewed by Dore did not have closer ties to neighbors than to their other acquaintances.

The maximum number of neighbors known to a single family in a British working class housing estate was found to be five—three in one direction and two in the other.[32] The same number is reported for an American sample of married women.[33] The number of neighbors known is not only small but spatially confined to a few houses nearby or to a portion of a street. Unfortunately, the information on the frequency and extent of neighboring is barely enough to make any but the most superficial comparisons and assessments. Even the terms "closeness" or "frequency" are not always consistently or explicitly defined. Nevertheless, the pattern suggested is that where neighboring is informally practiced, its scope and range are highly restricted.

Intensity of Neighborly Relations ▪

All studies agree that there are varying degrees of intensity in neighbor relations, ranging from a knowledge of neighbors' names to exchanging polite greetings to more intimate personal relations. Similarly, neighbors may only occasionally consult one another or may habitually count on each other in times of need; they may borrow and lend tools and money freely, or they may pay lip service to being neighborly without ever letting it come to a test.

Intensity is partly a function of the collective definition of neighboring prevailing in an area, and partly, especially where such binding definitions are lacking, of the emotional and economic needs of individuals. Some people do not like to be dependent on others under any circumstances while others use the smallest pretext for fostering such dependency. These attitudes reflect the characteristic stresses of one's milieu, of whether people live in an environment of self-sufficiency or of continual crisis. In an atmosphere of self-sufficiency it is the request for help that is morally frowned upon, whereas in a crisis-ridden environment it is the refusal to help that is condemned.

The most careful exploration of intensity of neighboring[34] suggests that intensity may be inversely related to extent or number of neighbors known. The authors could not study extensity as such because they confined their study to limited samples of twenty households in each area selected. Within these limits, however, they discovered the existence of a number of different patterns.

The measured intensity of neighboring for the 500 households studied was estimated by the authors to be rather high. Out of a maximum total score of 6.00, the modal intensity score was 1.00 and the median 2.20— possibly because of the slight overrepresentation of households of relatively higher socioeconomic status. These scores conceal a number of different area patterns of neighboring. There is the tribal pattern, where neighbors are enmeshed in a diversified round of exchanges and contacts; the intimate pattern, where families are involved with only a few of their neighbors; the casual pattern, where a series of overlapping contacts link many families to one another indirectly; the clique pattern, where there is a dominant group and many isolated families; the ring-around-the-rosie pattern, in which every family has one or two contacts but there is no indirect network linkage among them; and finally the anomie pattern, in which isolation of families from neighbors and neighborhoods is the rule. The origins of these patterns were not clear, and the attempts to correlate these patterns with residents' characteristics failed.

GENERALIZATIONS ON NEIGHBORING ▪

In sum, we have little precise but enough piecemeal information on each of the separate dimensions of neighboring to suggest the need for the systematic study of all of these dimensions on a large enough sample and in various settings. Only in this way can the loose and unintegrated propositions about intensity, frequency, occasion, and extent of neighboring be properly tested. The following generalizations, based on the studies consulted, must be interpreted with caution, but they do provide a starting point for a more systematic investigation.

1. *Content of neighboring activities*. Neighbors are turned to in situations of crisis of a minor or a major sort. This may involve borrowing a utensil to prepare the evening meal or fighting a fire. Neighbors are also sources of useful information about each other or about common problems. These activities—of exchange of help and of information—seem to be stressed wherever neighbors are expected to maintain any sort of relationship at all.

2. *Priority*. In less urbanized settings neighbors appear to be consulted less often and for less serious problems than are relatives but somewhat more often than are friends. The suggestion emerged that with urbanization immediate relatives replace distant relatives and friends replace neighbors as sources of help, information, and social ties.

3. *Frequency of contact*. Here our knowledge is sparse, especially when dealing with urban populations

for whom neither the occasions, range, intensity, or amount of neighboring are formally specified.

4. *Intensity and extensity.* Neither range nor depth of neighbor relationships appear to be very great in urban areas, although there is considerable individual and group variation. Most people do not know many neighbors, nor do they know them intimately. Neighbors here stand somewhere in between the closeness of blood relatives and that of personally chosen friends. In areas of much contact among neighbors, neighbors know more about each other because of the overlap of kinship, friendship, and neighborhood ties. Similarly, more people in such areas know a great many neighbors by sight and name, but this is due less to personal interest or concern than to the general setting that makes this knowledge virtually unavoidable. According to F. Zweig, the "intensity of neighbourly contacts can be graded in this order: (1) villages; (2) old established working class areas; (3) new estates; (4) residential quarters in own house property." [35]

5. *Formality.* In general, the more essential neighbor relations are for the functioning of areas or communities, the more formal, rigid, clear-cut, and firm these relations are likely to be. As the need for these ties weakens due to increasing individual and family self-sufficiency, the ties also become less formal. Thus, urban settlements are less likely to have formal neighbor relations than rural areas, big cities less than small towns, and the more urbanized areas within cities less than the less urbanized areas within cities.

6. *Locale.* This dimension makes sense only in urban areas where the integration between place, work, and folk is either diminished or lacking entirely. Different

groups develop different patterns for the locale of neighboring, some preferring their homes, others the street or local meeting places.

These dimensions appear to be interrelated to some as yet unmeasured extent. In highly urbanized areas with rising standards of living the priority, frequency, formality, and intensity of neighbor relations decrease in favor of relations with the immediate family and personally selected friends. The content of neighbor relations is still geared to crises, but the crises have diminished in number and altered in kind as alternative solutions displace neighbor cooperation to a considerable extent. A loosening of interlocking networks of obligation, cooperation, and shared experience accounts for the declining role of neighbors as intermediaries between the collectivity and its members. It is in this sense that Cooley considered the neighborhood as a primary setting in which collective emphases and local needs are each given due weight, exerting a reciprocal influence that results in a better mutual alignment. In cities, where neighbor relations assume a more subjective character, this chain relation is disrupted, and, except for a few areas of traditionally high neighboring, individuals are not linked to a larger collectivity by the mere fact of neighboring. This is because in cities neighboring becomes a segmentalized activity; however, in villages and small towns it is part of a comprehensive web of interlocking relations and dependencies of gossip, work, worship, and recreation where people know one another not only as social actors but as individual human beings. In cities the circle never quite closes in this way, not only because of the changed tempo and temperament of urban men but also because urban power and influence are not confined to the local milieu.

In sum, this review of the various dimensions of neighboring suggests the following generalizations:

1. Neighboring is a socially defined relationship ranging from highly formalized and institutionalized rules and obligations to highly variable, voluntary exchanges.
2. In essence, neighboring involves exchanges of services, information, and personal approval among those living near one another, however nearness is defined.
3. The needs prompting these exchanges may be divided into four categories:
   a. The daily, unexpected occurrence that is unforeseen yet recurrent, such as running out of bread or needing to post a letter.
   b. The big emergency, such as a fire, illness, or death.
   c. The significant collective event—marriage, birth, a holiday.
   d. Cyclical collective needs—as at harvest time, during economic depressions, and during job layoffs.
   The aid exchanged among neighbors is both material and spiritual.
4. Neighboring exhibits varying degrees of intensity and frequency although our knowledge here is extremely meager.

Neighboring also has different manifest and latent functions. Its manifest functions (those explicitly and overtly intended and acknowledged) involve the exchange of moral and material aid, including tools, information, and advice, in times of minor and major crises. Here neighboring helps meet certain recurrent needs of a population that are not met by the formal institutional machinery. From this a number of additional or latent functions of neighboring derive. One of these is the exercise of reciprocal social control to help sustain common standards and shared communication without which the necessary help during crises may not be forthcoming—either because neighbors might not concur in their definitions of what constitutes a crisis or agree on appropriate ways for dealing with it. A second latent function is to supply and spread information, quickly and efficiently, via gossip, throughout a given area. Gossip chains are channels for the diffusion of information that is officially unacceptable or censorable (being of a private or personal nature) and yet a useful addition to the general storehouse of collective intelligence about the membership. As such, it is an important resource during manifest crises when this fund of "forbidden" knowledge may profitably be drawn upon. In addition, gossip, or the transmission of scandalous information, reaffirms the distinction between respectable and disreputable conduct and thus helps promote latent consensus on manners and morals. And thus a third latent function of neighboring is the creation and maintenance of social standards of correct belief and conduct. Only by communicating with others do individuals learn the accepted rights and wrongs of their milieus. In old-established communities this helps reaffirm accepted standards and thus contributes to social integration.

In newly established communities as well as in the more heterogeneous urban areas most observers have noted a distinct change in the effective functions that neighbors are able to exercise. Though they may still wish to exert social control over each other's behavior, they have lost the power to do so in view of alternative sources of companionship and economic sustenance. In More's *Utopia*, as Meyerson has pointed out, a person "was under constant observation by his neighbors and the magistrates, not only during his work hours but also in his leisure time, so that he could spend it correctly." [36] Such surveillance has comparatively little impact in modern cities where moral disapproval, without the backing of social and economic sanctions, has lost much of its sting.

If urban neighbors have lost their powers to control each other's behavior, they have not altogether lost their importance as standard bearers. In the newer communities it is precisely to their neighbors that newcomers look for clues as to how to behave and what goods to acquire. Here neighbors may become a key reference group, and certain pace setters among them, in fact, may enjoy great influence for a time. [37]

The findings reviewed thus far suggest the following hypotheses:

1. As crises diminish in number and kind, where, that is, self-sufficiency increases, neighbor relations will diminish in strength and significance.
2. As new forms of social control arise, the significance of neighboring as a means of social control will recede in importance.
3. Where neighboring is a segmental activity in an open system rather than an integral part of a closed system, it will be a highly variable and unpredictable phenomenon.

4. Since all three conditions are more true of urban than of pre- or suburban areas, neighboring should diminish in extent, significance, and stability in cities.

PATTERNS OF NEIGHBORING: SELECTED EVIDENCE ■

Many different factors determine whether or not, how often, and for what purposes neighboring occurs. These factors may reinforce each other or work at cross purposes; they may be independent or interdependent. The discussion in this section is intended to supply a general guide rather than to exhaust the multiplicity of detailed conditions and considerations at work in a particular case. One way of classifying the diverse influences affecting rates and patterns of neighboring in settlements is to separate the traditions of neighboring in stable settlements or regions from patterns emerging under conditions of social change.

TRADITIONS OF NEIGHBORING ■

Rural-urban patterns. People generally try to conform to the patterns of conduct around them, and many people engage in neighboring activities and relations simply because they are expected to do so, because this is the way things are done in their town or district. To understand the attitudes and conduct of individual neighbors, therefore, one must know the standards of neighboring current in their environment and how they vary. In general, the social structure of a settlement affects the kinds and amounts of neighboring occurring within it.

In the small, rural village with long-established traditions, a common way of life, an intertwining of work, family, and social relations, and a common destiny, neighboring is a by-product of life itself. People need not engage in direct contact to know about one another since opportunities for indirect contact abound. Their interdependence binds them as much as or more than any genuine personal attachment. The absence of alternative opportunities puts a premium on mutual aid, sociability, and support in time of crisis and strongly encourages local loyalties. Not that this by itself automatically results in local harmony. Everyone knows of the tensions and rifts, the jealousies and conflicts that disrupt the façade of many a tranquil town, but these personal struggles, while determining the quality of social life, do not fundamentally alter its basic pattern. The sociology of village life makes neighboring mandatory.

In cities this type of neighboring, according to all accounts, is mandatory no longer. It survives in particular, often villagelike, settings within the urban framework where the need for mutual aid, social solidarity, and personal sociability is strong. Those sections of the urban population that most resemble their village counterparts also most resemble them in their way of neighboring—although this way is never entirely unmarked by the urban stamp. Ethnic minorities, immigrant colonies, working class enclaves and even middle class suburbs in a somewhat different sense show a marked inclination and need for neighboring. If these groups are also physically immobile—far from rapid means of transport, too poor to afford them, too overworked to find much use for them, incapable of finding their way in the teeming urban centers, or afraid to face unfamiliar people and places—their neighboring will assume the familiar spatial form.

But here, as in the villages that serve as implicit models in many planning schemes, neighboring is more than a purely personal matter. It is itself an institution, connected with and supplementing other institutions. Individuals are no more free (though the degree of this varies) to give or withhold neighborly contacts than they are free to neglect their children, their work, or their other moral duties.

In general, it appears that the more self-sufficient a community and the more self-reliant an individual or a group, the smaller the reliance on neighbors and the weaker the traditions of neighboring—with one notable exception. Sometimes at extreme levels of poverty where self-interest has not been effectively linked to collective purpose, where distrust, suspicion, and fear mark the relations between man and man and between man and community, we find nothing resembling the neighboring that we have described because we find nothing resembling the society that gives rise to it. What we do find is a truncated, impoverished, anomic form of life in which every man is out for himself, his spouse, and their young (not grown-up) children. This life survives mainly because outsiders carry on, via force or idealism, the collective tasks the inhabitants will not or cannot assume.

The often assumed decline of neighborly relations in cities may be traced in part to changing definitions of and changing needs for neighbors. For many urbanites the range of this relation in heterogeneous urban areas probably does not extend much beyond the dwellings adjoining one's own on either side, and the relations maintained with these adjacent tenants may not go beyond noticing such superficial facts as when they enter or leave their homes, whether they make much or little noise, and whether they have many or few visitors. As collective definitions of neighboring loosen, individuals are freer to define the relation as they see fit. The perception of the neighbor as helper in times of need, as friend, as harmless occupant next door, as irritant, or as enemy will then determine the relations ensuing among them, and these perceptions will vary by subculture and class, and as tempers and tastes vary.

In urban centers both the solidary and the anomic variety of neighboring may be found—from the transient, anonymous rooming-house residents, who pick up stray relations when and where they find them, to the stable, solid citizens, who stick close to home in all things. Some have referred to these as urban villagers; and in a sense they are, for many of them actually were brought up in villages. They then transfer their habits and outlook to the urban habitat and cut them here and there to fit the urban cloth. This helps counteract "all those forces which tend to make city life anonymous and atomic—the rapidity of residential change, the increase in secondary contacts, the tendency for man's primary contacts to develop on occupational lines and to be independent of territorial propinquity. . . ." [38] Social origins and traditions of particular groups and individuals thus account for one kind of neighboring in urban areas. Current social class affiliations account for another.

Social class. The amount, the extent, the intensity as well as the occasions for neighboring seem to reflect social class. We might sum up the established, and not always consistent, findings with the terms "working class solidarity," "middle class selectivity," and "suburban sociability." In solid working class areas of skilled and semiskilled workers, need and limited opportunity, isolation and relative poverty, insecurity and fear of outsiders, all combine to make neighboring an essential part of the close web of family, kin, and work relationships. Often this neighboring is neither selective nor personal but rather a generalized expression of attachment to the local area—its shops and taverns, its streets and residents—promoted by common problems of economic uncertainty and often in conjunction with particular ethnic and cultural traditions.[39]

In middle class milieus neighboring takes on a different form. Above all, it is more selective, more personal. And personal compatibility comes to matter as much as occupational and cultural compatibility. Greater economic well-being decreases the need for mutual aid and increases the use of critical, selective faculties. At the same time the pursuit of competitive success accentuates the importance of social status and makes selectivity more necessary. In the words of one writer, "the higher the level of prosperity, the higher the fences." [40]

Opinions vary about the actual amount of neighboring in middle and working class milieus. Some studies suggest that middle class families engage in more neighboring than lower class families, while others find just the reverse. It depends on the particular aspect of neighboring stressed. Intensity of neighboring was positively related to higher socioeconomic status in San Juan. "Prosperity, not misery, loves company. Sociability declines as the need for support and assistance increases." [41] We must keep in mind, however, that the concept of neighboring used in the San Juan study was essentially social in content based on the nature of informal relations among urban residents. It ignored that aspect of neighboring that some consider primary— mutual aid in time of crisis—and that appears to underlie neighboring in traditional working class areas. There is agreement that middle class neighboring is more selective, personal, or intimate and more likely to involve next door neighbors. Moreover, in middle class settings families blend neighborly with social and recreational activities, and neighboring is thus more home-centered than is working class neighboring. The latter is a compound of necessity, isolation, and relative deprivation, which is as much a cry for help as an expression of mutual friendliness and goodwill.[42]

Physical isolation and economic need have thus been used to account for characteristic working class patterns of neighboring. Economic depression, unemployment, and the shifting fortunes of local industries made workers and their families extremely dependent on one another—especially where alternative public assistance measures were nonexistent or inadequate.[43] Along with this there is the fact of a concentration and an overlap of significant common experiences. "It is only in the working class," observes Bott, "that one is likely to find a combination of factors all operating together to produce a high degree of connectedness: concentration of people of the same or similar occupations in the same local area; jobs and homes in the same local area; low population turnover and continuity of relationships; . . . little demand for physical mobility, little opportunity for social mobility."[44] "People courted, mated, married, quarreled, and amused themselves in a confined area from which escape was difficult—financially, geographically, and emotionally." But note that this neighborliness generally occurred under conditions of "physical drabness, economic stringency, and bodily contiguity. The scope for personal choice of any kind was very limited." [45]

Once the scope for personal choice increases in response to higher living standards and opportunities for physical and social mobility, the traditional, rural, and working class type of neighboring tends to decline. Bott observes that in the transition from village to urban life the generalized propensity for neighboring is transformed into a more selective set of attachments in urban areas.[46] So it is not social class as such but a general loosening of dependency on place and people that accounts for rural-urban and for working-middle class differences in neighboring.[47]

It appears, then, that neighboring, as indeed any other social activity, is socially structured and somehow adapted to the type of community and setting in which it occurs. Rates and patterns of neighboring vary between town and country, slums and suburbs, transient and stable districts; all of these in turn reflect particular economic conditions, levels of cultural and recreational activities, and local standards of sociability. On this overall, normative level we find that neighboring is more extensive, solidary, and generalized, and in that sense de-individualized, in the solid working class areas, the small cohesive villages, and the homogeneous new communities, where need combines with fellowship to make neighbor relations almost as close and nearly as necessary as family relationships. In contrast to these, the middle class areas of solid comfort and greater occupational and cultural heterogeneity are marked by neighboring that is more selective, less intertwined with other aspects of life, and more likely to emphasize personal sociability and compatibility. Less crisis-oriented, it is also less utilitarian than its traditional working class or rural counterpart.

Within this overall framework other factors such as individual and group values, age, sex, personality characteristics, and individual ambition and status awareness come into play. They affect the extent to which given individuals and groups will in fact conform to the general standards current in their environment. However, these factors are usually subordinate to the broader standards, working within and alongside the primary determinants, and do not exert an independent influence on them.

SOCIAL CHANGE AS A FACTOR IN NEIGHBORING ■

Ours is an era of rapid social change in values, institutions, and the mentality and behavior of individuals. Under its impact old patterns of neighboring decline, and in time new ones emerge. In the interval individuals, groups, and entire communities must cope with transiency, instability, and a certain amount of normlessness. Depending on personal resiliency and social traditions, individuals either succumb to these pressures or successfully resist them by eventually establishing a new equilibrium.

The social changes affecting the amount and kind of neighboring may be divided into three kinds: (1) general changes in values and institutions; (2) changes in the manner of life for individuals and groups—due to residential and social mobility; and (3) changes through time—both for individuals and for new communities.

General change in values and institutions. The changes commonly associated with industrialization have resulted in a radical reappraisal of fundamental institutions and values, including love, marriage, friendship, and, of course, neighborliness. Improved standards of living, increased physical and social mobility, and greater self-sufficiency of individuals and families, in short, trends that decrease dependency on local, traditional settings, and increase selectivity in work, recreation, and social life also decrease reliance on neighbors. As the range of physical and social mobility increases, traditional bonds are loosened and, if not discarded, at least critically reappraised. Whatever is retained of the old forms is rarely kept intact; it is altered to suit the new conditions of life. Thus, wherever the long process known as the industrial revolution has started, there we note revolutionary changes in family organization, work associations, political patterns, and cultural and recreational activities. These changes often result in great moral anxiety, but usually the human spirit reasserts itself, forges new bonds to men and to places, and establishes a new morality, which may, in time, suffer a similar fate.

Once the network of traditional standards is broken, there is, of course, the danger that the more heterogeneous, individuated population that must now fend for itself can no longer achieve the consensus needed for collective life. Once the traditional web is loosened, not by the individual maverick or misfit, but in varying degrees by all who were previously bound by time and destiny, there may be no halting the disintegration of the entire frame. Although this opens up new horizons, new doors to adventure and experiment, it also creates a new breed of man, each following a different drummer and dreaming a different dream.

The decline of a general consensus goes hand in hand with a decline in a general, standardized morality and the power of its collective representatives. Where each is freer to live as he chooses, the opinions of neighbors carry less effective weight. Social disapproval is, of course, still unpleasant, but it is far less scathing a weapon than it was in the villages and towns of an earlier era. The very same forces that have decreased the need for mutual aid among neighbors have also undermined their power to control one another's manners and morals.

Secondary institutions and associations arise to replace local neighborhood ties in emergencies as well as in day-to-day life. Birth clinics, marriage bureaus, social insurance schemes, and public assistance in various forms link individuals directly to the larger community. Changes in the organization of production, scientific and technical advance, and specialization of work, all decrease the capacity of local institutions to meet changing needs. Local solidarity thus declines even in districts where it was strongly developed:

For all that some nineteenth-century working-class neighborhoods had, at their best, valuable qualities of warm human relationships, they were—and are—grim places in which to live and especially in which to bring up children. . . . Organized society found itself obliged to step in to protect those who, individually, were helpless or who

needed equipping for useful life. First came compulsory
health measures, then compulsory schooling, then very
limited free school meals, then rehousing, then compulsory
slum clearance, then educational reorganization, then free
nutritional policies for all, and so on.[48]

In Tokyo, despite its formalized neighboring etiquette, fire insurance, life insurance, and post office
savings schemes became widely employed and loosened
dependence on neighbors. Even under dire stress there
is now less need for neighbors and, with the greater individualism of urban dwellers, perhaps less likelihood of
finding a helpful response among them. The reliance on
alternative sources of assistance is matched by a reliance
on alternative sources of social contact. Even among old
and relatively immobile tenants in a group of apartments
especially designed for them, who would seem to need
immediate neighbors with whom they share their old
age, physical infirmity, relative isolation from relatives,
as well as economic poverty, we find that they do not
depend greatly, and certainly not solely, on neighbors
for emotional and social sustenance.[49]

Occupational heterogeneity in neighbourhoods, houses better equipped for leisure than neighbourhood areas, more
women working, less knowledge of each other's changed
occupational and economic activities and less common experiences as a result of them, plus individual ambition for
themselves and their children, all reduce the sense of fundamental and inescapable equality among neighbours.[50]

The reasons for the decline of neighbors and neighborhoods as primary sources of material and moral support may be summarized as follows:

1. The presence of multiple sources of information and opinion via mass media, travel, voluntary organizations, and employment away from the local area.
2. Better transport increasing mobility beyond local village or district boundaries.
3. More differentiated interests and desires as well as differentiated rhythms of work resulting in a lowered inclination to neighbor unselectively. This also results in lesser amounts of shared free time available for leisure.[51]
4. Better social services and greater prosperity and economic security.

These changes, affecting solidary working class districts in cities no less than solidary small towns and rural villages, result everywhere in a decline of organized as well as spontaneous neighborly associations.

Change in family type. Thus, general social changes usher in changes in all aspects of life as the new challenges and displaces old patterns, habits, and institutions. Among the latter, the reorganization of the family institution is of paramount importance—in particular the shift from the extended type with sharply segregated sex roles, male dominance, and strict authority relations between parents and children to the smaller, companionate type of family with greater equality and shared interests among all members. This type of family, reflecting a growing individualism and self-sufficiency, is also better suited to the demands posed by physical and social mobility. Concentrated as it is on the most essential, immediate, and irreplaceable human ties, it reacts more selectively to its environment and achieves a certain independence from it. The consequences for neighboring are quite predictable. These companionate families are able not only to be selective in their neighboring but also to forego neighbor relations altogether, not because their needs are fewer but because they are different and better met by alternative institutions to which individuals relate on the basis of membership, not on the basis of place.

As the opportunities for choice multiply, moreover, people choose not only their clothes and their houses but also their spouses to suit personal taste. They thereby establish a highly individuated and personal relationship. Where family relations followed traditional standards, rooted in written or unwritten law, the personal aspect played a less decisive role. But as the family becomes a smaller, more flexible unit, founded by choice and dissolvable thereby, subjective factors assume greater significance. In fact, the relationship survives only to the extent that the partners make it live. To do so they must concentrate on it and on each other. As Simmel has told us, a potentially tragic quality marks all relationships that need two persons for their formation but may be destroyed by only one of them. Therefore, it should come as no surprise to find that this type of family, in which the partners relate to each other not only as role partners but also as unique individuals, turns in upon itself, becoming home-centered and highly selective in its social relationships.

All the so-called warmth and fellowship of the slums did not ever make the slums a home-centered society. Husbands and wives had different interests and pursued them in different places. Rather, the slum society was one of "the extended family, the street, the alleys, and the neighborhood." Eating together provided the main occasion for common family activity. Each member was "emotionally identified with the area, the women in the mutual exchanges of the kindred and in the gossipings of their neighbors, the men with their cronies on the street corners, the bar, or the allotment. The children form their own play groups." [52] People were friendly with the neighbors in a general, diffuse way. Few were friendly with the neighbors next door.

In the villages, too, we note this escape from family and wider kin obligations into local taverns and associations for recreation and emotional release. Where duty is emphasized, individuality must always take second place. But as the individualism fostered by urban industrialism extended to the family sphere, these relations took on a new character. The greater individuality of the partners gives them more to talk about with each other and more opportunity for individual self-expression in the home. Greater intimacy between husbands and wives makes it less necessary—in village and city, in Tokyo no less than in New York—for either partner to seek solace among neighbors. And as Bott points out, it *is* possible in cities to have no informal relations outside the family. One can work, use some service institutions, and visit a few relatives a few times, and for the rest withdraw, quite happily, to one's own foyer.[53]

All of these—the withdrawal to the home, the greater individualism, the decline of local institutions, and more variety in tastes, means, and standards—set off a spiraling process in which the greater heterogeneity among neighbors decreases their collective impact, which in turn decreases their personal and social interdependence, which further reduces their influence and potential for consensus.

We may summarize the chief impact on neighboring

of the wider social changes ushered in by industrialization and the accompanying urbanization as a shift from a neighboring of *place* to a neighboring of *taste*. Greater self-reliance, alternative ways of meeting individual and collective needs, greater economic security, more individuality decrease the significance of neighbors as sources of mutual aid in times of emergency and as sources of social and emotional gratification. The degree to which the general social changes affect neighboring in specific instances, of course, depends on the differential rate and impact of these changes on different social groups and social classes—some groups being quite insulated from them, others being very much part of them.

CHANGES DUE TO PHYSICAL AND SOCIAL MOBILITY ▪

Increased physical and social mobility goes hand in hand with urbanization and industrialization. Migration from rural to urban areas as well as residential mobility within urban areas becomes almost routine, affecting every class level of the society.

Individual responses to a move. In moving from one region or place to another much more is at stake than the tedious and unsettling process of being in transit. Unless the move is to another dwelling within the same general area, it also means disruption of old friendships, school adjustments for the children, and changes in transportation and shopping habits, all of which demand a great many additional subtle personal adjustments. Unless people move in groups, they must usually leave behind their old neighbors and relate to new ones. How they do so will depend on the traditions of neighboring from which they stem, their own individual responses to the move, and the conditions that await them in their new surroundings.

It has been found that even if people move to areas inhabited by others much like themselves, moving provokes tension and anxiety. There is the problem of unfamiliarity with the physical setting. There are the problems of not knowing how to behave in an environment where the old standards may not apply and new ones have not yet been established. There is also the initial feeling of loss of the community left behind and the loneliness in the midst of strangers.

One response, noted in many new towns and housing estates, is the "retreat to the home." Husbands may take a new interest in working around the house and garden. Husband and wife may draw closer together in their strange new environment, and this, added to all the other changes affecting family relations, contributes to a new companionship between them at least during the initial period of stress and anxiety. This is true even for working class residents who were previously neighborhood-centered rather than home- and family-centered.[54]

In addition to changes within the family, newcomers appear also to turn to next door neighbors for companionship. Comparing two roughly comparable working class groups, one that had stayed in its old neighborhood and one that had moved to a new housing estate, Mogey found that the housing estate residents showed a less rigid division of labor between husband and wife, somewhat fewer meetings with kin and distant relatives, much more likelihood to have friendly relations with the next door neighbors, more likelihood to have more than one friend, and more associational affiliations other than with the Church.[55]

At first people may seek out someone from their old environment. This occurred on one British housing estate where a new family apparently preferred to go for help to an unknown, former, old neighbor than to a strange, new, next door neighbor.[56] But if a family fails to find old neighbors in their new environments, they will have to relate to new neighbors. This is not without strain and false starts for many families, and adds to the overall difficulties occasioned by the move—hidden and unexpected expenses, increased indebtedness as a result of credit buying, and family problems as each family member is differently affected by the move. Thus, the reactions of people to their new setting and new neighbors "can vary in pattern all the way from close, confident neighborliness through uncertain association and superior contempt to nervous, withdrawn isolation." [57]

Group responses to a move. In part groups will carry their traditions of neighboring with them. For example, people "who have lived at close quarters—for instance in Glasgow tenements—are less shy of their new neighbors than those who have lived in separate dwellings." On the other hand, "people used to the vast impersonalness of London are shy of closer contacts which life in the new town implies." [58] Social class background likewise affects the reactions to the move and the sorts of communities established. In middle class suburbs, for example, the more status-conscious white collar and professional families are highly selective in their social contacts with friends and neighbors. Interested in community improvement and in associational activities, they take a much more active part in creating the sort of world they want. In striving to maintain, assert, or improve their status, they pay particular attention to their surroundings, valuing privacy, good education, supervised recreation for their children, home ownership, and nice neighbors in nice neighborhoods. Their well-described gregariousness, thus, has its well-defined limits. Working class suburbs, on the other hand, are quite different. They reflect some basic characteristics of working class residents in general: fewer organizations, fewer and poorer facilities and schools, better sports facilities, more pubs and taverns, and a social life largely concentrated on relatives.

For both groups neighboring takes on a new form but one which cannot be understood without reference to the environment left behind. Thus, Gans observes that for middle class individuals there is actually more neighboring in suburbs than in cities; for working class people there may be less.[59] Popular impressions notwithstanding, the suburbs are neither uniform in their social characteristics nor in the patterns of neighboring they exhibit.

Of course, to the extent that the general social changes previously described have affected and thus altered traditions for both the working and the middle classes, to that extent will their neighboring change in their suburbs. With a rise in the standard of living, made possible through mass production and credit buying, men become more individualistic and self-reliant, more selective and mobile in their search for competitive success. The continuous confrontation with strangers who must be judged and who will judge one by outward appearances increases status anxiety. In many new communities the increased preoccupation with external symbols of social status—houses, cars, money, clothes, appliances—has been noted. For the less resourceful whose status anxieties make them imitate patterns far beyond their means this may mean growing financial indebtedness, insecurity, and other associated problems, all part of the price of moving.

Thus, physical mobility has no uniform effect on neighboring. Culture and social class each play their part. For example, Bracey noted a tendency for English newcomers to remain apart from others for a much longer period than American newcomers despite the fact that Americans were more mobile and had alternative amusements and diversions available.[60] Working class residents on new housing estates or in suburbs show less generalized neighboring, a retreat to the home, more selectivity in choosing friends and acquaintanceships, and a preference for next door neighbors if no familiar faces are around. Middle class residents in new suburbs, always more selective, have been shown to engage in more neighboring in their new environment and may even be somewhat less selective for a time.

Much depends on the conditions confronting the newcomers in their unfamiliar settings. The environment to which people move affects neighboring principally in two respects: (1) the facilities available for amusement and diversion and (2) the social composition of the new community. If people move to a new community that lacks many essential facilities and services, they either turn to immediate next door neighbors or find themselves completely isolated. Lacking shops, taverns, churches, and centers as well as established social networks, these unfinished communities produce many hardships for newcomers.[61]

The social composition of the new community also seems to play a crucial role. "In general where newcomers have much the same traditions and customs, settling down is easier than in communities of mixed origins." [62] When people feel they know "who" the people around them are, it is easier to agree on standards and to establish consensus and people are less suspicious. This is another reason for wanting "to live among one's own kind." Where this is not possible, housewives have been known to join a community association for the sole purpose of making acquaintances "without committing themselves to undue intimacy with neighbors." [63] It also avoids that pressure toward external conformity so common on new estates and so likely to cause internal stress and anxiety. Where there are formal mechanisms to integrate newcomers in an area, the strains and trials of the move are much diminished. The formal etiquette of neighbor relations in Japanese cities provided rural migrants with such a framework and thus indirectly with a model for urban living, particularly among the women who generally bear the main burden of such a move.[64]

The strains of the move are mitigated in large part by the actual or perceived social homogeneity of the population in a new environment. When working class people move into mixed areas, they seem to feel the weight of status inferiority and discrimination and respond by withdrawing to their own immediate families and a small circle of kindred spirits. When they move to a socially similar area, there is less defensive isolation.

Similarly, middle class families moving to middle class suburbs, elated at having fulfilled their social aspirations as well as their desires for more space in nonurban surroundings, socialize and organize with great enthusiasm during the initial period there. But gradually, a sorting out process begins, and subtle selective factors reassert themselves to make for more discriminating neighboring. When middle class families find themselves side by side with those they consider inferior, they either join community associations in the search for more congenial company or they strive to leave the community as soon as possible. The inferior group, resentful at this presumption of higher status, then either withdraws or becomes overtly hostile. Middle class residents have no monopoly on social snobbery, however—any assumption of social status exclusiveness will result in separation or hostility among groups, isolation, or awkwardness among individuals. Naturally, in all of this, personal and chance factors may affect these general tendencies and result in exceptions to the general pattern.

Phases of Neighboring in New Communities ▪

Disraeli's famous and often quoted remarks about the absence of communal bonds in the new towns in his own day were premature. He did not, as he thought, describe a permanent condition but only a temporary phase in the transition from one way of life to another, as the uprooted, unsettled, atomized wage earners became "accustomed to town life, took its measure, learnt its disciplines, established ties with neighbors, and built up life around the chapel." [65] This was especially true among the respectable working class elements. This should make us cautious about premature generalization, such as that concerning another frequently noted phenomenon—the so-called "friendliness" of middle class suburbs where families appear to engage in a round of visiting, gossiping, and organizing all around the clock, or the "apathy" of the working class suburbs. As we shall see, neither working class apathy nor middle class euphoria are permanent collective states.

Two phases of neighboring and socializing may be identified according to available data on communities in transition and on new communities. The first phase is characterized by eager interaction and mutual helpfulness, whereas the second is characterized by restricted interaction, selectivity, and withdrawal.[66] These phases are particularly in evidence on middle class housing estates and in the suburbs, but they have also been documented for some new working class estates whose residents have developed more middle class ambitions and tastes.

Originally, it was thought that the physical layout and design of suburbs, their small size and low density, were conducive to high sociability. Later this view was revised with the suggestion that suburbs may simply consist of self-selected people, people who moved into them with the precise intention to find congenial neighbors with similar habits and outlooks. The self-selection is actually twofold: middle class people can afford to buy or rent houses in the suburbs so that more of them congregate there, and within the middle class suburbs attract those who particularly value what suburbs have to offer. Nevertheless, even suburbanites pass through an initial phase of indiscriminate neighboring which does not last.

Among the values people may seek to maximize by moving to suburbs, neighboring has high priority. This is the substance of Fava's findings in one of the few studies that provides direct evidence on this point. Comparing three socially similar samples from a central city, a peripheral area, and a suburban area, she found that migration to the suburbs "differentially attracts those who are willing to neighbor." [67] This willingness is reinforced by the social similarities among suburbanites as to age, family cycle, and occupational interests. There is also the stimulus of the pioneering spirit of newcomers engaged in a common enterprise, which may initially make them more tolerant of individual differences. These similarities in values, purposes, and styles of life may make superficial relations proceed smoothly at first; but once deeper personal characteristics are touched, relations may reveal discordances and dissimilarities not conducive to enduring personal ties. The initial phase is, therefore, marked by a superficial, transitory, and, in a way, depersonalized intimacy.

The precise reasons why this initial phase does not last are not clear. After all, the social characteristics of suburbanites do not change nor, presumably, do their values regarding the desirability of suburban living. Available data suggest that in time social status differences and a more discriminating urban mentality make themselves felt. Social class and status distinctions, however fine, reemerge and affect informal neighboring that, in these settings, tends to involve home entertaining; and home entertaining is generally more status-involved than socializing outside of the home. Furthermore, new social status distinctions appear either as a result of job and career changes or of renewed status strivings among the more ambitious residents. Such factors as where people take their vacations, what new appliances they acquire, how many cars they drive, how often and whom they entertain, and more subtle preferences revealed through longer acquaintance may become the basis for new status discriminations.

As individuals and families become absorbed in community associations and activities in which they participate according to specialized interests and abilities, the urban pattern with its greater impersonality, its secondary relationships, and its individuation superimposes itself on the suburban setting. "Having passed this initial stage with its pioneering outlook acting as a temporary mask to the basic urban pattern, the suburbanite once again turns to the urban way of life both in his individual and family relations." [68] Privacy then becomes important both as a means of establishing status boundaries and as a way of conserving time.[69]

It is interesting to speculate about the observed differences in this second phase as it affects working class and middle class suburbanites. Both types appear to pass through an initial phase of intensive, indiscriminate neighboring, though perhaps this is less true for working class residents, especially those compelled to move. However, it is especially in the second phase that class differences emerge. The middle class residents appear to turn outward to the larger community to participate actively in its cultural, political, and associational life; the working class communities turn inward, their residents withdrawing to their own homes and families, venturing forth little if at all. Lacking certain traditions, skills, or perhaps interest, they do not readily establish these wider community links. It is, therefore, in these communities as well as among those middle class individuals personally incapable of wider participation in the community that one notes the characteristic complaints that have often been attributed to suburbia in general, complaints of isolation, loneliness, apathy, the new town blues, and the nostalgic yearning for lost homes. Thus, Mogey points to the paradox of an old working class district being considered by its residents to be a friendly place despite the fact that it showed a very low acceptance of next door neighbors, whereas a new working class housing estate was heavily criticized for being a cold and unfriendly place despite its very high acceptance of next door neighbors. He suggests that in the old districts more people are known vaguely by sight and gossip and there is less dependence on physical proximity for human contact. In the new housing estate, however, everything is strange—the house, the layout of the estate, the way the streets connect, the faces of the people, the children, and even one's own behavior. Also there is no way, at the beginning, of obtaining indirect knowledge of the people on the estate.[70] If people cannot adjust to the new setting, they move away, and such moves are most frequent in the early period of the formation of new housing estates.[71]

Thus, the following consequences for neighboring may result from a move to strange surroundings: (1) separation from the old and isolation and strangeness in the new; (2) a frantic period of neighboring to counteract the difficulties of the move, the inadequacies of the setting, or personal anxieties; (3) a settling down process followed by a retreat to the home and selective attention to neighbors in working class districts and a branching out to community-wide associations and activities in middle class ones; the latter leading to (4) a more urban texture of life in the middle class suburbs or among those actively participating in the community whatever their backgrounds and a more provincial reaction in working class suburbs or among families tending to withdraw into their own narrow worlds. Time thus plays a crucial role in neighboring and must always be considered when evaluating a particular community.

INDIVIDUAL AND GROUP CHARACTERISTICS AND NEIGHBORING ■

Since carefully designed, systematic studies of neighboring are virtually nonexistent, research findings often appear to be contradictory when they may only be reflecting differing definitions of terms or research procedures. In view of these limitations, the empirical findings presented here are suggestive rather than firmly established. Future studies should hold constant social traditions, social class, and phase of neighboring so that the role of such factors as sex, age, personality, and family cycle may be properly assessed. All of these factors have been shown to be related to neighboring in some manner although to which of its several dimensions or in what measure is not yet clear.

For example, both children and older citizens, more than other age groups, have been found to draw their social contacts from among neighbors. Small children are said to bring neighbors together, but they are also the most frequent cause of argument and dissension among adults either because they engage in quarrels or because they interfere with adult interests and needs.[72] Recognizing that children are one of the information links among households, adults may keep family secrets from children.[73] The propensity among the elderly to select their friends from among neighbors may be due either to age as such or the length of residence in an area, the two often going hand in hand.[74]

It is generally thought that women, especially young women with children, are more involved with neighbors than are men who find their companions among their colleagues at work. This has not always been true, however. In rural German villages men used to be the neighbors *par excellence* since women were tied to their households.[75] And in San Juan, Puerto Rico, middle-aged women were more likely to engage in extensive neighboring; the size of the family played no significant role.[76]

Social status shows an inconsistent relation to neighboring patterns. An exception to the widely accepted and well-documented finding that lower income groups, minority groups, and rural migrants are more neighbor-oriented than the better off, higher status elements comes from the study of San Juan. Here the families with more intensive neighboring relationships had good education, high income, and comfortable homes, had lived in the area for some time, and were above average in their social participation and church attendance.[77]

Finally, some suggestions on the role of personal predispositions may be gleaned from the existing literature. Such traits as whether a person is introverted or extroverted, pugnacious or kindly, dependable or irresponsible may determine whether he wishes to establish contacts with neighbors and whether they wish to do so with him. Some effort has been given to classifying people into types, such as local and urban, that may have a bearing on their neighboring behavior.[78] These types, emerging in appropriate social settings, are equivalent counterparts to the social structure. Since personality is not always in harmony with the broader environment, however, they may also emerge in environments antithetical to them, as when urbanites develop within rural communities and parochial types in urban areas. Dobriner fashioned a ten-item Likert-type scale based on the qualitative distinctions associated with these character types and tested it on a sample of suburbanites. He found suggestive, though preliminary, results in the expected direction.[79]

We do not as yet know whether one or more of these dimensions—personality type, age, sex, and social status—overlap and thus reinforce each other. If men are more likely to be "urban" types than women, middle class individuals more so than lower class individuals, and younger inhabitants more than older ones, then districts, estates, or communities consisting of young, middle class families will also be more "urban" in orientation than those composed of older, working class families. And if women should turn out to be more of the "neighbor" or "local" types, they will decrease the urban score for both samples.

The final factor to be considered is that of physical design.

PHYSICAL DESIGN IN NEIGHBORING ■

There are two principal ways in which physical planners have tried to affect social relations among neighbors—

one, by decreasing the physical distance; the other, by decreasing the functional distance between neighbors. The physical distance among residents may be reduced by increasing densities or by improving accessibility through better means of transportation. Functional distance may be reduced by a number of architectural and siting devices, such as the facing of dwellings, the siting of stairways and front and back doors, and the location of bus stops, footpaths, landings, and roads.

Except under very special conditions, however, the manipulation of physical and functional distance does not have an unequivocal impact on social life. Even where the reduction of physical and functional distances leads to increased visual and personal contacts among residents, this may not be followed by increased sociable contacts among them, and when applied to incompatible groups, it may even increase interpersonal friction.

PHYSICAL DISTANCE AND SOCIAL CONTACTS ■

Physical distance registers through the senses as one hears one's neighbors and is heard by them, sees them entering and leaving their houses or walking down the street, or stares into their rooms opposite one's own. Physical distance may be reduced by bringing the observer closer to the object or the object closer to the observer or by increasing densities in a given space or by mechanically bringing voices, sounds, and images nearer via radio, telephone, or television. As such it undoubtedly affects certain aspects of social life. For example, residents in a subunit of a British housing estate, intensively studied by Kuper, knew, in the sense of being

able to name, two-thirds of the residents in their subunit but only one-sixteenth of those living outside
them.[80] The smaller the area involved, the larger the
proportion, though not the number, of names known.
As for social relationships, the same held true, but the
magnitudes involved were smaller. Within each subunit, only 14 percent of all possible social relationships
were claimed. These findings compare favorably with
those of Festinger, Schachter, and Back's earlier study
of a postwar veterans' housing project in Massachusetts
in which physical distance had been found strongly related to friendships among residents.[81] On the basis of
such studies of friendships, marriage rates, and residential segregation, it was somewhat hastily concluded that
physical distance is directly related to the formation of
friendships, to rates of marriages among potential partners,[82] and to the preservation of "the social heritage
and style of life of the varying subcultural units within
the society as a whole." [83]

Recent studies, however, have increasingly challenged
these claims. Physical distance as such is no longer
considered sufficient to account for the formation and
perpetuation of social contacts, especially of a more enduring sort. There are many instances of physically compact units, streets, and areas where residents, though
physically close, do not establish any relationships with
one another.[84] Something more is clearly involved when
they do form such relations.

FUNCTIONAL DISTANCE AND
SOCIAL CONTACTS ■

It is not enough that people are physically near one
another; something must bring them into contact, pref-

erably into inadvertent or "passive" contact as a natural by-product of routine activities such as entering or leaving their homes, going shopping, or waiting for transportation service. These inadvertent contacts may at first lead to nothing more than visual recognition, then perhaps to some polite greetings or formal exchanges about the weather, and eventually to more personal relations. This notion, introduced in the aforementioned study of the postwar veterans' housing project is conveyed by the term "functional distance." Functional distance is affected by such factors as the siting of houses, their ecological location at a corner or in a central place, and shared uses of facilities (for example, stairways, footpaths, or lobbies). On the basis of carefully collected data, the authors of that study hypothesized that the smaller the functional distance between residents, the greater the number of friendships formed. Kuper carried this work a step further when he presented data for a different, and heterogeneous, setting. For example, he found that, contrary to expectation, tenants in houses facing one another did not develop friendships despite their physical proximity. This was due to the fact that the front of the house was not fully regarded as living space, the houses being "physically oriented toward each other, but not functionally." The real functional link here turned out to be between the side houses, and the good neighbor in this subunit was likely to be the side (in a separate unit) rather than the party (attached unit) neighbor even though the party neighbor was physically closer.[85] Both naming and sociable contacts occurred more often with regard to side than to party or other neighbors. And, as was true in the study of veterans, the ecological location of the houses was likewise significantly related to certain indexes of sociability.

The significance of functional distance of relations among side rather than party neighbors was reflected in the residents' complaints. Only one of these, noise, was intrinsic to the house itself and, naturally, involved party neighbors more. The remaining complaints, such as the placing of side doors, the low windows of the living room, and the position of access paths, arose from the grouping of houses and the siting of their essential features.[86]

Functional distance is not necessarily conducive to friendships, however. There is evidence to show that decreasing physical or functional distances may increase hostility among those brought nearer to one another.[87] Still other evidence suggests that siting, design, and physical or functional distances are irrelevant to social life,[88] except perhaps insofar as knowing or recognizing neighbors may be easier in relatively small places or in places with relatively few people, especially when they use common facilities.[89] Superficially, this may increase visual recognition among residents, as it does even in the large metropolis for those consistently shopping in the same grocery, stationery, or department stores. However, any more personal contacts are rarely the result of such inadvertent encounters. As Riesman has pointed out, "the encounters of people are psychological as well as ecological and . . . of course, creative contact is not simply a matter of numbers and chance encounters." [90] We may here recall the study of Lower Overbrook in West Philadelphia where common facilities did not lead to a greater sense of community among their users.[91]

Other things being equal, differences in physical and functional distances may well influence social contacts and relations in that the closer the distance between two or more residents, the more likely they would recognize one another by sight, sound, and, perhaps, name. We cannot say the friendlier they would become because they may not go beyond these superficial contacts. In some instances, however, these superficial, physically maneuvered contacts do develop into more enduring personal relationships. The reasons for this must lie in the fact that physical distance and siting do not play an independent or a "determining" role in social relationships.[92] Something intervenes to minimize or maximize their influence. These intervening variables may significantly alter the direct impact of physical factors on social life.

INTERVENING VARIABLES ▪

Time, layout, ecological position, social similarity, and compatible moral and social standards are the chief intervening variables.

Time may minimize the importance of siting and distance in some respects and increase it in others. Gans, for example, feels that physical proximity is important for the initiation of contacts; but for their perpetuation and maintenance other factors come to the fore.[93] Similarly, Festinger, Schachter, and Back feel that time conquers distance in that as one becomes more familiar with an area and its facilities, one extends one's range of contacts so that the number of friendships formed in small and in large communities gradually becomes more equal.[94]

Gans also suggests that physical proximity may play a less significant role for some activities than for others. Impersonal social activities, such as card playing, may well be sustained by residents living near one another, whereas discussions and intellectual exchanges will require special characteristics that may make people search for contacts farther afield.[95]

Many have argued that physical design and siting become significant for social relations only when a certain, as yet unknown, degree of homogeneity and social similarity has prepared the ground for it. Where people feel that those living near them are their own kind—having similar personal and social standards, similar ambitions and aspirations, and similar family relationships—physical proximity may permit or encourage (it never guarantees) sociability. This is the substance of the findings of veterans' housing projects and student communities. As Gans has summed it up, propinquity brings neighbors into contact, but it is because of homogeneity that this contact is maintained on a positive basis. And Schorr has formulated an analogy to Boyle's law for social interaction: the physical space that neighbors occupy is inversely proportional to the likelihood of interaction among them—but only in the new, planned, and fairly homogeneous communities. Where communities are stratified, decreasing physical distance among socially unequal neighbors may lead to hostility between them. In these views social homogeneity helps promote "a congenial social atmosphere," whereas social heterogeneity is accompanied by conflict and dissatisfaction.[96]

In this connection it is interesting to compare the facts of the two best studies on the subject, the veterans' study in Massachusetts and Kuper's study of a subunit in a Coventry housing estate. Each study found functional distance to be closely related to the formation of friendships despite the fact that the veterans' project was highly homogeneous, the British subunit, highly heterogeneous. At first glance this would appear to confirm the case for the independent role of functional distance in social relationships. However, more careful inspection of the findings show that though these communities differ as to homogeneity, one major factor is similar: in both cases the residents are all newcomers. We have already noted how the fact of being among strangers promotes the formation of next door neighbor relations in both homogeneous and heterogeneous communities but seemingly for different reasons. In the heterogeneous setting the fear of differences drives newly arrived residents to seek some human contacts with immediate neighbors and even to make concessions to their differences because of their dependence on them. In the homogeneous setting it is simply more convenient to make friends nearby than far away. This a point that puzzled the authors of the Massachusetts study when they observed that although the average distance from one door to the other in one of their projects was only about 20 feet, the number of friendships, nevertheless, decreased steadily as distances widened. The men in these buildings all went to the same school and had many other interests in common; "yet," the authors note, physical and functional proximity proved to be crucial. The point is that the "yet" should really read "therefore," for it is precisely because all these other factors were equal that the law of least effort could prevail. It is only where they are not equal that people will forego convenience for the sake of compatibility. It may also be noted that despite the circumstances favorable to the formation of friendships on a physical distance basis, not all residents formed friendships on this basis even here.

Thus, social and cultural similarities, roughly equal social class standing, similar personal needs and desires for neighborly relations, certain kinds of activities, and duration of contacts may counteract the effect of physical and functional distance on sociability. These intervening factors have been summed up under the terms social homogeneity versus social heterogeneity. Recently, however, these global terms have been criticized for oversimplifying and even distorting the issue since homogeneity is not a constant but a variable and is thus a matter of degree. Also, since social life is many-sided, a group may be homogeneous with respect to one set of factors but may be heterogeneous with respect to others. How, then, is one to arrive at an overall estimate of the group's homogeneity? Since there are so many differences to be taken into account—with respect to values, social class ranking, social origins, life-cycle stages, and personal experiences—how is one to add them all up, and according to which criteria can one decide that there is "much" or "little" homogeneity? Even if one could determine the extent of the homogeneity, there is evidence to suggest that the homogeneity-heterogeneity dimension is not necessarily the most relevant one. Except at the extreme points of the social hierarchy, social differences need not work against friendly or neighborly interaction provided that the potential partners are personally compatible. That is to say, shared attitudes toward neighboring irrespective of social affiliations are the crucial determinants of social relations within a given physical space. Since there is no one-to-one correspondence between a given group or class affiliation and attitudes toward neighboring, individuals may have similar attitudes to privacy, open space, entertaining, and sociability despite differences in cultural and social characteristics. Similarly, within the same group or class attitude divisions may subdivide the group into several incompatible factions. Thus, Kuper notes that the status division between the rough and the respectable was significantly associated with neighboring, these distinctions occurring within a fairly homogeneous working class group of residents and reflecting varying shades of respectability within that class.[97] Perhaps, as he suggests, passive contacts resulting from decreased functional distance may actually play a more significant role in heterogeneous groups precisely because they make possible encounters among a few likeminded people in the heterogeneous setting.

Consequently, it may not be social homogeneity so much as personal compatibility that proves to be the decisive intervening variable between physical distance and sociability. Of course, the two generally go hand in hand; only during periods of rapid social change may we expect a striking imbalance between group membership and social attitudes and values. However, it would seem that even where the two roughly coincide, the finer the measuring rod used, the subtler and perhaps more meaningful the discriminations one can make. Manual workers are not all alike, varying in social background, current income, style of life, family composition, tastes, and experiences. Some of these differences may be more significant for neighboring and friendship than their overall similarities. The same holds true for any other social category. Where these differences of class, status, and style of life are neglected, we find friction, withdrawal, high rates of out-movement, or continual strife among physically proximate residents. In fact, in such cases intimate layout and carefully planned "passive" encounters may actually promote instability. Kuper notes, for example, that just as respectable families will tend to avoid contacts with their less respectable neighbors, so the sociable residents may quickly move away from very reserved families. "Reserved families are often ideal tenants from the point of view of a housing manager, and probably the very last he would suspect as a cause of high residential mobility." [98]

Certain groups depend more for their social contacts on physical proximity than others. Housewives with young children, the old and infirm, the immobile and the poor may be so eager for any kind of social contact nearby that other considerations are held in abeyance or do not come into play. But one may also argue that because of their greater personal need, physical distance is actually irrelevant to their social relationships. This may explain why the poor are likely to be block dwellers who use space inclusively compared to the better-off who are likely to be selective city dwellers.[99] However, once so-called block dwellers are uprooted from their familiar habitats and joined with strangers whose habits differ from their own, they also become more selective.

Thus, physical design as such—in the sense of arranging dwellings and facilities so as to encourage personal encounters followed by more enduring personal ties—does not seem to play an independent role in neighboring. It is significant primarily where social and personal compatibility has prepared the ground for it. This compatibility may have its source in social status or cultural similarity, shared attitudes, ideological tolerance, or some sort of complementary rather than conflict-arousing differences.

Even in special cases where intergroup contacts were carefully planned around common facilities and siting features so as to help promote mutual understanding and good will, the norms of intergroup contacts proved more decisive than physical proximity as such. In their famous study of interracial housing Deutsch and Collins found that integrated housing projects did show more social contacts and more mutually favorable attitudes between Negro and white housewives than was true for the segregated housing projects. However, this was due neither to physical nor functional distance since both the integrated and the segregated projects had tenants equally near or distant from one another.[100]

"The siting factors, with their planned and unplanned consequences," writes Kuper, "only provide a potential base for neighbour relations. There is no simple mechanical determination by the physical environment." [101] Even carefully planned facilities permitting chance or passive encounters designed to reduce functional distance (such as bus stops, food shops, or laundries) may be "engineered" if someone wants to avoid someone else.[102] Thus, we have no basis for claiming a consistent, and certainly not an automatic, role for the effects of physical distance and design on sociability.[103]

CONCLUSION ■

In sum, the provisional classification of factors affecting neighboring is as follows:

1. Traditions of neighboring by place and social class, with small town, rural, and ethnic or immigrant enclaves in urban areas placing greater reliance on neighbors than the larger, more heterogeneous, more urbanized settlements. As for social class, here too, characteristic patterns emerge according to the life-situation of particular classes and their prevalence in different environments. Working class solidarity has been contrasted with middle class selectivity and two phases of suburban sociability.

2. Social change as reflected in changing values and institutions and in increased physical and social mobility.

3. Individual characteristics such as sex, age, family life-cycle, personality, and character type.

4. Physical design provided it takes into account the social and personal composition of a given population.

These factors or dimensions have in a sense been "teased" out of the data, and need to be established by systematic, carefully controlled research.

2 The Neighborhood

The term "neighborhood," most investigators agree, is not without its ambiguities. Essentially, it refers to distinctive areas into which larger spatial units may be subdivided, such as gold coasts and slums, central and outlying districts, residential and industrial areas, middle class and working class areas. The distinctiveness of these areas stems from different sources whose independent contributions are difficult to assess: geographical boundaries, ethnic or cultural characteristics of the inhabitants, psychological unity among people who feel that they belong together, or concentrated use of an area's facilities for shopping, leisure, and learning. Neighborhoods combining all four elements are very rare in modern cities. In particular, as we shall see, the geographical and the personal boundaries do not always coincide.

The common elements of most definitions of neighborhood are territory and inhabitants. Ruth Glass describes a neighborhood as "a distinct territorial group, distinct by virtue of the specific physical characteristics of the area and the specific social characteristics of the inhabitants." [1] It is easy, she observes, to find neighborhoods that are distinct territorial groups, but it is difficult, especially in cities, to find neighborhoods whose inhabitants are also in close social contact with one another. In rural areas, neighborhoods in both senses were easier to locate. Their characteristics have been summarized as follows: places with a name known to their inhabitants and smaller in size than a community, having common facilities such as a general store, a grist mill, or a school, and marked by social relations that include the exchange of assistance and friendly visiting.[2] These are still the chief dimensions considered in urban studies. Ideally, residents of different neighborhoods are marked by a particular pattern of life—the subculture of their district—whose norms will reflect the type of terrain occupied, the dominant type of land usage, the social traditions, and the general socioeconomic structure of the area. All of these elements operate within "flexible but real geographic bounds." [3]

Although there is some agreement on the core elements of the concept of neighborhood, "there is great variability in the totality included in it." [4] Since the physical and the social components of neighborhoods are those chiefly stressed, let us consider each in turn.

PHYSICAL COMPONENTS ■

The neighborhood, viewed as an area or a place within a larger entity, has boundaries—either physical or symbolic and usually both—where streets, railway lines, or parks separate off an area and its inhabitants or where historical and social traditions make people view an area as a distinctive unit. Usually these two boundaries reinforce each other: the physical unity encourages symbolic unity, and symbolic boundaries come to be attached to physical ones.

In either case a neighborhood is marked off from other neighborhoods in some distinctive and recognizable manner and thus has an ecological relation to the rest of the community. The location of the neighborhood and the qualities associated with it give it a certain value in the eyes of its residents and the community at large. This value is based on whether the area is conveniently or inconveniently accessible to essential activities such as work, shopping, schooling, and recreation. The rating of each neighborhood is a function of the availability of these services and of their importance to the individuals affected.

Some physical characteristics of a neighborhood, such as the layouts of streets, houses, and landmarks, are independent of its ecological characteristics. Concentrations of buildings, land use and facilities and their accompanying impact on densities, dwelling conditions, the presence or absence of light, air, and green open spaces, give an area a spatial and aesthetic identity and texture. The quality of such basic services as water supply, police and fire protection, and sanitation determine both the level of comfort and the reputation of an area. Here, too, the neighborhood is in some significant respects judged by the standards of a larger area whose capacities and preferences it reflects in miniature.

Neighborhoods are formed only under certain social and ecological conditions. One can hardly speak of neighborhoods in most villages since these are so small and familiar to their inhabitants that the whole community might be considered one neighborhood. With growth in size, the number of people, or the variety of services, the whole becomes subdivided into subareas with characteristic functions and local significance. Neighborhoods and their particular configurations of services, activities, and people thus exist precisely because a city or town has been so subdivided. The nature of these subdivisions, their uniformity and variety, are determined by the nature of the totality and its degree of specialization in work, tastes, and standards of life.

SOCIAL COMPONENTS ■

Within its physical and symbolic boundaries, a neighborhood contains inhabitants having something in common—perhaps only the current sharing of a common environment. This gives them a certain collective character, which affects and reflects people's feelings about living there and the kinds of relationships the residents establish. It also contributes to the reputation of an area, which even more than its potential for fellowship and convenience may weigh significantly with its more status-conscious residents and determine their relative contentment with the area as a place in which to live.[5]

Sociologists are more likely to stress the importance of the symbolic and cultural aspects of neighborhoods and take the physical features more or less for granted. What particularly interests them is the meaning attributed to an area by its occupants and users. Spatial and physical attributes strike them as necessary but not as sufficient conditions for the existence of neighborhoods. In contrast, physical planners tend to consider the physical aspects as primary. The sociological conception of neighborhood emphasizes the notion of shared activities, experiences, and values, common loyalties and perspectives, and human networks that give to an area a sense of continuity and persistence over time. Residents of a neighborhood are seen to share a special and somewhat unique destiny arising from their ecological position in the city, their ties of past and present, and their general orientations toward the area and to one another. It is clear that the sociological conception is best realized in the more traditional rural communities or in certain social and cultural enclaves within a larger urban area.

Summarizing the two prominent conceptions of neighborhoods, we arrive at the following, sometimes incompatible, dimensions:

1. A physically delimited area having an ecological position in a larger area and particular physical characteristics arising from natural geographic conditions and from a particular configuration of activities and usages. The work of the "Chicago School" refers to these as "natural areas." [6]

2. An area containing such facilities as shops, clubs, schools, houses, and transportation that may be used by those living in the area or by outsiders. In the latter case a neighborhood has a special functional role in the organization of a town or city. Investigators do not always distinguish between these two types of usages—by residents and by outsiders. Some consider usage of neighborhood facilities as an index of the existence of neighborhood only if this usage is exclusively confined to residents. Yet, if outsiders

use a particular neighborhood for recreational, business, or cultural purposes, this itself may be a significant determinant of neighborhood identity.

3. An area representing certain values both for the residents and for the larger community. Such values as cleanliness, quiet, safety, social solidarity, political cohesion, ethnic or religious compatibility, aesthetic quality, and social prestige have different priorities for different individuals and groups and are present in different measure among the subareas of a community.

4. A field or cluster of forces working in and on an area to give it a special atmosphere. An immigrant ghetto, a middle class suburb, or a skid row area has a special aura that affects how the area looks and how people look at the area. In part, this is an inscrutable phenomenon, and like the personality of an individual, it cannot be reduced to the composite elements since it is an outcome of their interrelations. Each individual and activity contributes to this collective effect even while they are subordinate to it. Areas thus have collective records on crime, delinquency, residential stability, wealth, morale, and morality. Neighboring is only one of the activities and components contributing to this collective record.

All of these somewhat different aspects have been included in that one term—neighborhood. No wonder that this complicates systematic discussion and inquiry.

METHODS FOR ASCERTAINING THE PRESENCE OF NEIGHBORHOODS ■

The existence of separate neighborhoods in urban areas has been studied in two principal ways, using either ob-

jective or subjective indicators. Using the objective
method the investigator identifies and locates physically distinct areas on the basis of statistical and census
data, physical reconnaissance of the terrain, and information supplied by informants deemed especially knowledgeable about the area. Thus, Glass, in her pioneering
efforts, plotted distributions of selected indicators of
such area characteristics as net population densities,
age and conditions of dwellings, ethnic and religious
composition of the inhabitants, occupations, and figures
on school attendance. She then noted where these over-
lapped. By tracing boundaries around areas of concentrated or overlapping distributions, she was able to
identify twenty-six potential neighborhoods.[7] More recently, a study in West Philadelphia, seeking to locate
subareas for more intensive analysis, asked twenty-one
well-informed local persons to "name the areas which
they thought of as neighborhoods." Newspapers, historical accounts, and organizational records provided sup-
plementary information. Eventually, it was possible to
identify sixteen areas ranging in population from 10,000
to over 40,000 persons.[8]

An alternative approach utilizes information about
where the people of a given area shop, work, and play,
and the spatial distribution of these activities provides
the basis for the drawing of boundaries. In earlier investigations of village neighborhoods, for example, areas
were marked off according to the uses of village centers;
usually this left some marginal areas unaccounted for
and therefore unclassifiable. Instead of asking adults
where they shop or work, one may ask school children
attending particular schools where their parents go for
certain services and then plot their answers in relation

to their individual residences. A variant of this technique is to obtain the addresses of clients, members, or customers from village stores, schools, weekly newspapers, and churches, and then plot these service areas to see whether and where they overlap.[9]

Another main approach asks respondents themselves to indicate the boundaries and extent of their neighborhoods.[10] Often this method is used in conjunction with the first and serves as a check on its utility.[11]

ASSESSMENTS OF FUNCTIONING NEIGHBORHOODS ■

Even the most ardent partisans of the neighborhood as a purely spatial phenomenon would agree that the location of geographically demarcated areas is no proof of the existence of actual neighborhoods. Some additional information is usually considered necessary to ascertain whether the residents in such areas also perceive them to be distinct social and symbolic units. Thus, Glass, having identified twenty-six distinct territorial groupings, went on to consider whether these also exhibited a given degree of concentrated social activity. This involved a comparison of the geographic units with the "catchment areas" of the following facilities and services for degrees of boundary coincidences: the catchment areas (that is, the spatial distribution of members) of all elementary and secondary schools, of youth and adult clubs, of post offices, and of greengrocers and shops for sugar registration.[12]

In an intensive study of three West Philadelphia subareas previously identified as possessing some neighborhood potential, the following dimensions were studied further to see whether this potential was being realized: identifiability of the area; identification with the area; presence of friends and relatives within the area; use of local stores, churches, and recreational facilities; attitudes toward the area; and presence of organized local groups for the handling of local problems.[13] Another investigator participating in this broad inquiry into local neighborhood life selected twelve subareas by means of social area analysis, a technique used to locate distinctive subareas of larger census tracts. This investigator asked one hundred randomly selected respondents in each of these subareas to identify the subarea by name and boundaries and to evaluate the area as a place to live.[14] The study, in not preselecting its neighborhoods, has an advantage over those that do. There does not exist an inadvertent concentration on areas of known neighborhood potential. As a result, however, this study, as well as the one by Glass (which it resembles in some respects), found very little overlap between potential neighborhoods and actual neighborhood identity, use, and participation.[15]

A knowledge of the prevalent social character of an area, ascertained by various indexes of living conditions, residential stability, and population characteristics, may be used as clues to its neighborhood potential. If we know, for example, that a given area has a high concentration of home owners of particular income and educational levels in skilled manual occupations, we might estimate their neighboring activities to be low on the basis of what we generally know about neighboring in such groups. Or, the presence of certain facilities may reveal the sort of population with which we are dealing. Pawnshops or secondhand stores may signal the presence of low income groups; selected churches and schools, that of high income ones. In fact, Baltzell suggests charting the presence of certain schools and churches as a convenient way to trace the neighborhood migrations of fashionable society and thereby the rise and decline of fashionable upper class neighborhoods.[16]

Information about boundaries, use of facilities, or relations among neighbors in particular areas does not tell us how adequate, suitable, or desirable such local areas are. For this, objective standards or yardsticks are required. Since such standards are lacking, relative comparisons (for example, ranking areas according to the presence of certain facilities) and unstandardized subjective judgments are most frequently used, but neither of these permit us to generalize. The two questions most frequently used to tap neighborhood satisfaction are: (1) Do you consider this neighborhood of yours a good place to live? and (2) Do you intend to remain in this neighborhood permanently? [17] The answers to these questions, whose precise meaning is not always clear, are then correlated with other characteristics of the respondents, the area, or both. Sometimes, instead of a single question, several questions are used, and an index is constructed.[18] Or a more refined attitude scale with several ratings for each item may be devised. Individuals may also be asked to describe their conception of an ideal neighborhood or to choose among several photographs of neighborhoods the one that they prefer. A series of "games" has been designed that probe into people's wishes and attitudes regarding neighborhood facilities and services.[19] For example, respondents are given fixed sums of money and are asked to imagine what facilities and settings they would choose for a house they had won, or they are asked to select among a series of density figures and commuting patterns those they prefer. In analyzing how they "spend" the money at their disposal, their values and preferences are thus revealed.

ESTABLISHING BOUNDARIES OF NEIGHBORHOODS ■

The extent of neighboring in an area is an unreliable clue to neighborhood boundaries in a rapidly changing urban area since not all people rely on neighbors; if they do, they have contacts with very few of them. If neighborhoods were to be defined by people's attachments to neighbors, the areas delimited thereby would be too small and variable to provide either general standards or areas sufficiently large for systematic planning purposes. Moreover, person-to-person neighboring is at best only a partial datum. People may not engage in neighboring and yet make use of local areas in other ways. Most investigators and planners would, therefore, include a wider area in their conception of neighborhood. But how wide? If it is possible to have neighborhoods in which little or no person-to-person neighboring occurs, then how are these neighborhoods to be demarcated?

Various attempts to solve these problems have so far not met with any great success. In the aforementioned study by Glass and her co-workers, only five of the twenty-six physically distinct subareas showed any overlap between physical and institutional or service boundaries. This suggests that the utilization of various urban facilities is dispersed and "not carried out within the boundaries of distinct territorial groups." [20] The five that did exhibit a concentration of social activities within the territorially delimited area did so for all the reasons that planners regard as undesirable in a neighborhood—isolation, social class homogeneity, and poverty.

Such physically clear-cut dimensions as size of area or size of population also prove unreliable indicators. Glass found that the population of the twenty-six territorial entities was quite irregular, ranging from very few to more than 10,000 people. Similarly, the *barrios* of San Juan also vary greatly in size.[21]

Subjective demarcations are likewise unreliable guides —when people are asked to draw the boundaries of their neighborhoods, few of them draw identical ones. And when asked to state the name of their neighborhood, they often do not use the one officially used by outsiders for the area or district. In two southern cities of the United States, for example, fewer than one of ten respondents thought of "this part of town" as "having any particular boundaries or limits." And only three-tenths "supplied some kind of neighborhood name in response to the question: 'If someone you meet elsewhere in Greensboro asks you where you live, what do you tell him?'" The author concluded that people have a rather imprecise notion of neighborhood as a smaller part of the city.[22] When asked to designate a name for an area, people do not always use the most widely known or used name even though they may recognize it if they hear or see it.[23] In the West Philadelphia study, referred to earlier, it was found that the area name used by the informants, neighborhood associations, and social workers was not universally known by the inhabitants of the area, seven-tenths of whom considered the area simply as part of West Philadelphia in general.[24] In a racially mixed area in the same city a particular name was adopted for its prestige value, thus representing a "case of the extension of a prestigious name to a less prestigious area." [25] In contrast to these findings Ross reports that two-thirds of the residents of an old-established area of Boston were able to supply the conventional name of the area, and four-fifths were able to name three of its four natural boundaries.[26] But only three-tenths of the 379 residents interviewed in Stevenage, a British New Town organized into six "neighborhoods" of about 10,000 inhabitants each, were able to give the proper name of their neighborhood despite the fact that the Stevenage Development Corporation had placed great emphasis on stimulating neighborhood identity.[27]

It appears, then, that people do not generally identify the subareas they live in by name or distinct boundaries unless such areas are either geographically or socially isolated or have a definite class or historic identity. People do, however, identify by name and boundaries fairly small subsections of their areas, often including no more than the street on which they live. These may more properly comprise neighborhoods as they see them.

Many studies suggest, however, that even small subsections may be quite differently perceived by residents reporting on their experiences and activities there.[28] Even a single street may be cut up into tight little islands where exclusive and often antagonistic groups form separate units, manifesting neighborly kindness and generosity within them but distance and hostility between them.[29] Under certain conditions one finds a public opinion of the street that controls personal behavior both inside and outside the home and lays down local standards of taste and conduct to which the residents must conform.[30] West Philadelphia residents when asked to describe their "neighborhood," would indicate:

the street and block on which they live. . . . These areas are usually no larger than a single block of facing houses between two cross streets. When we asked respondents what area they really knew, they usually limited themselves to a small area, seldom exceeding two to three blocks adjacent to their own house.[31]

Similarly, in Stevenage, previously cited as an example of residents not knowing the names of their neighborhoods, respondents named their housing estates instead, suggesting that if they identified with a residential area at all, it was likely to be much smaller than the designated neighborhood, containing a population nearer 2,000 than 10,000.[32] Gans provides other supportive evidence when he notes:

[The] concept of the West End as a single neighborhood was foreign to the West Enders themselves. . . . The residents divided it—the area—up into many sub-areas, depending in part on the ethnic group which predominated, and in part on the extent to which the tenants in one set of streets had reason or opportunity to use another.[33]

These small, "natural" neighborhoods find their limits where personal relations stop. This makes their boundaries fluid, though still recognizable to those familiar with local customs, and responsive more to psychological and social factors than to physical ones, recalling Simmel's observation that nearness and distance have more to do with the state of one's soul than with the nature of space itself.[34]

These examples suggest that physical factors appear to be significant only in conjunction with social factors and do not seem to exert an independent influence on neighborhood identification. In fact, physical factors may even be subordinate when respondents subdivide their street according to the social status characteristics of the various inhabitants. As Gans has noted, the strong local identification of the first generation ethnic immigrants was not related to common residence on the block or in the slum but to family and ethnic ties.[35] The social texture of a block may be highly significant in other groups also. One detailed study shows this to be the case among British manual workers who lived in three separate blocks of twelve houses each. Each family was interviewed by one investigator. The blocks were remarkably similar in social composition, consisting of young families of manual workers who had lived on the block for more than a year. Closer scrutiny revealed some block by block differences. Thus, Block One included both a clerk and a member of the factory staff among its residents, whereas Block Two included only workers at the shop floor level, and Block Three contained more suburban families with a slightly wider range of occupations among the husbands and a larger number of children per family. Of the 36 families, only 11 stated that they had good neighborly relations involving mutual assistance; 14 had little contact with neighbors but were not critical of them; and 11 had either no contact or unwanted contact. The variations by block were considerable. In Block One 9 out of the 12 families had either no or poor neighborly relations, whereas in Blocks Two and Three the majority had either neutral or positive relations with their neighbors. Ten of the families were strongly critical of the housing estate and wished to move away, another 10 were somewhat critical, and 16 were satisfied and intended to stay. The families on Block One were most dissatisfied.[36] This study shows very clearly how complicated are people's interrelations within a very small space indeed. Even people as similar in objective social characteristics as these were found to be quite heterogeneous in their responses to their immediate neighbors.

Today people are much more differentiated in their tastes, loyalties, and habits than is often assumed. In one working class district in central Oxford, for example, a local population of about 1,000 families supported sixteen public houses, "a sign that, left relatively free from municipal control, the size of these informal groups . . . is very small." This fragmentation of local loyalties contrasts strikingly with the single community center provided in the new housing estate, which these residents disdainfully rejected.[37]

As a result of the small subdivisions informally defined by urban residents, it is not surprising that people are vague or uninformed about the boundaries either officially established or geographically obvious to outsiders. Most people see and know only a portion of the area near them and they vary as to how big a portion that is. The demarcation of boundaries on this basis might be a first step in the ascertainment of functioning neighborhoods. Demarcation by use and sentiment are additional steps.

USE OF NEIGHBORHOODS ■

If a local area does not have great geographical or territorial distinctiveness, its inhabitants, nevertheless, may make concentrated and distinctive use of shops, schools, parks, and cinemas. This may not result in greater local pride or symbolic identity, nor indeed in greater neighborliness or emotional attachments to the area, but it may serve to link the inhabitants to one another and to the area indirectly through a sharing of these local facilities. This is surely the crux of most planners' justification for designing spatial subdivisions in a large urban area whose convenience and accessibility would help promote local utilization of services and indirectly encourage other local attachments and loyalties.

The concentrated use of local services and facilities varies widely according to the economic and cultural characteristics of the residents, the types of facilities and their adequacy, the accessibility of nonlocal facilities, and the degree of isolation of the area, economically, ecologically, and symbolically.

Of the many factors that may affect the local use of local facilities, we may distinguish between those factors concerning the inhabitants and those concerning the area, its services, and accessibility. The importance of social, economic, and ethnic status has been noted repeatedly. In general, persons in low income neighborhoods are more likely to require shops and services close to their homes.[38] In part this reflects their inadequate economic resources, but in part it may also reflect cultural and ethnic preferences. As Warner and Srole showed more than two decades ago, immigrant and ethnic minorities not only patronize local shops, churches, and clubs that cater to their special needs and habits, but their acculturation process may be traced thereby.[39] Status-consciousness may likewise inhibit or encourage the use of local resources. For example, in one working class housing estate the immediate neighborhood was avoided because of the existence of a rough crowd at the end of one road.[40]

Taste, access to transport, and sphere of activity must be taken into account when considering the facilities available. The adequacy of local facilities clearly affects whether or not people go outside their immediate district for the things they want or need. In Stevenage, prior to the completion of its town center, the day of the week made a great difference in the use of either local or town facilities. Although 85 percent of the inhabitants said they had shops within ten minutes walking distance, only 16 percent made use of these on weekends, whereas during the week, 60 percent made use of them.[41] The possession of an automobile may alter the perception of distance so that people who are within easy driving distance of certain facilities may consider them conveniently located.[42] Or, people may use a not too distant shopping area that is in the direction of the town center rather than one nearer to them in the opposite direction. The importance of physical distance decreases as various social, economic, and technological elements exert their influence. Families whose main wage earners work outside the local area, tend to make less use of local facilities than families both living and working within the area.[43] Here again, we note the variable role of physical distance.

Use of the local area also varies with the sphere of

activity. In West Philadelphia, McGough found that grocery shopping was more locally based than any other activity investigated. One-half of the respondents shopped for their groceries only in their own areas. The next most widely used "local" service was medical care, with from 40 to 60 percent of the residents going to physicians within their local areas. One-third to one-half of the respondents worshiped only in local churches. Only one-tenth worked locally, however. The author concludes that the use that residents make of local facilities is not related to such characteristics as class, race, or family size; rather, it seems strongly associated with the social mix of the area. In racially mixed areas, for example, she discovered a strong tendency for residents to go outside their areas for the satisfaction of their needs.[44]

The local area is clearly more important for some groups than for others. Just as intensive neighboring is closely correlated with conditions of relative helplessness or need, so the importance of the neighborhood seems to vary according to the resources of the residents. These resources may be economic, psychological, cultural, or ecological. Those immobilized by old age, family responsibilities, ill health, ignorance, or isolation need the neighborhood most, not only for the satisfaction of their tangible wants for goods and services but also for intangibles such as gossip and information. The traditional shops, cafes, and pubs in working class areas are also centers of information for their patrons. Some residents who may be quite isolated from human contact otherwise will, in this way, be kept up to date with local news and events. According to one observer, such individuals would quickly disintegrate if they moved to a new housing estate lacking such "news" centers.[45] The very young or old, the disabled and the overburdened who cannot venture very far from their immediate dwelling are really no more than "block dwellers," to use Schorr's phrase, in contrast to the young and relatively better off who are city dwellers and city users. The old and poor are "no more citizens of the city than was the kitchen maid of former generations a citizen of her mistress' house." [46] This is further confirmed by Glass and her associates, who found dispersal rather than concentration of activities "the very norm" in the twenty-six areas she studied, leading her to conclude that only a particular combination of negative characteristics, such as geographic isolation, poverty, and social homogeneity, made for any significant concentrated use of local areas.[47] This study also showed that the most prosperous neighborhoods ranked lowest on social integration as indicated by concentrated use of local institutions and services, a finding that perplexed the authors. On the basis of the present analysis of neighboring, we would say that since neighboring in general is directly related to self-sufficiency and fluidity, which are greater in the more prosperous neighborhoods, it follows that such neighborhoods should show the least concentrated use of local services.

NEIGHBORHOOD ATTACHMENT AND SATISFACTION ■

The three dimensions considered thus far—neighboring in an area, identifying the name or boundaries of an area, and use of area facilities—are not reliable guides to locating the presence of functioning neighborhoods, although each may be associated with this functioning in some manner.

Neighboring in an area cannot generally serve as a yardstick for determining physical boundaries because it is either too diffused and intertwined with many other activities, as in small towns or solidary urban districts, or it is too restricted and sporadic, as in larger urban centers. The extent and type of neighboring activity is mainly a function of the self-sufficiency of individuals and groups as reflected in their established traditions and practices.

Nor is probing for area names or boundaries of much help, since most people either do not have precise notions of such boundaries or they differ on the spatial referents of the names they use.

Even the use of local facilities and services is no sure guide to estimating the existence of coherent neighborhoods because most people do not use local services exclusively. They travel far and wide for work, shopping, and amusement. For example, grocery shops, most consistently preferred close to home, nevertheless show inconsistent use according to the day of the week, economic resources, personal mobility, and availability of alternatives. Some people are, of course, more confined to local areas than others, notably the physically handicapped, culturally isolated, or economically deprived, but even they are not irrevocably committed users of local facilities. The physically handicapped, moreover, are literally no more than house or apartment dwellers, and the culturally isolated will, in fact, travel some distance for their shops and churches if necessary.

There remains, then, a final dimension to be considered—that of attachments to some part of a local area.

Even if people have only casual relations with neighbors, even if they do not have a clear sense of the boundaries of an area, nor make concentrated or exclusive use of local facilities and services, they may have a special feeling for a given place, a special sort of pride in living there, a sense of attachment transcending physical inconvenience or social undesirability.

This attachment may be rooted in childhood experiences or family involvement with the area over a long period or in historical events endowing an area with a special meaning. It may also stem from current attractions such as the presence of favored friends, material or cultural advantages, or a particular aesthetic component. Any one or a combination of these may help tie people to a local place. And it is perhaps this feeling, this link, above all, that planners would like to inspire in the neighborhoods that they design.

Investigations of the degree and kinds of satisfactions with and sentiments for a local area are neither as wide ranging nor as systematic as one would wish. Nevertheless, some suggestive patterns emerge from the existing data. It appears that people are generally more satisfied than dissatisfied with their residential areas, although the precise meaning of satisfaction is difficult to ascertain.[48] It appears, moreover, that this satisfaction is indicative of a general outlook on life and is not substantially affected by specific local characteristics of an area. In certain areas of San Juan, Puerto Rico, for example, whose living conditions might strike outsiders as shockingly inadequate, residential satisfaction was high, seven-tenths of the respondents considering their areas as good places in which to live.[49] Although one-half of the Puerto Rican immigrants in New York City were dissatisfied with their living quarters, only 26 percent were dissatisfied with their neighborhoods.[50] Lest this be considered peculiar to Puerto Ricans, West Enders in Boston also indicated a strong attachment and sense of belonging to their area quite apart from their feelings about their dwellings.[51] Perhaps this illustrates an oft-noted tendency among working class people not to restrict their social lives to their immediate dwellings as middle class people tend to do nor to differentiate quite as sharply between private and public space.[52] Of course, much depends on what is implied by the expressions of approval. That they do not necessarily imply permanent loyalties to an area is suggested by one study. This study showed that while most of those interviewed considered their areas as a "fairly good" place in which to live, fully three-fourths could imagine living elsewhere.[53] One suspects that this would be far less true of residents in villages and small towns, especially in the less industrialized parts of the world.

Some of the studies cited hint at an important question, namely, the scale of place loyalties in the modern urban world. Such loyalties are not absent even in the large metropolis, but they do tend to adhere to fairly small areas adjacent to where one happens to live or work. Sprott suggests that this is implicitly recognized in Chinese villages and in Japanese cities, where neighborhood "cells" are very small, including no more than five neighbors on either side of a given house in the Chinese villages and no more than twenty households in the Japanese cities.[54]

It is difficult to know how to interpret these expressed attachments to local areas, whatever their size. Liking an area, as the following examples suggest, does not necessarily commit an individual to staying in an area or to exclusive or predominant use of its facilities and services. In one racially mixed area of Philadelphia both white and Negro residents appreciated the area for its cleanliness, quietness, convenient location, well-maintained property, and even the pleasant people. However, the white residents went outside the area for shopping and recreation and refused to participate in the single community organization, thus staying in the area physically but not in spirit. In Mantua, an area of San Juan having many social and economic problems, residents expressed liking for the area but felt no strong attachment to it. Alternatively, people may feel an identification with certain streets, shops, and other inhabitants of an area but fail to transform their individual loyalties into a general community spirit.

The expressed intention or desire to move away from an area has often been used as an index of attachment to it, but this overlooks those people who may stay in an area they dislike because of economic necessity or because they own property there, or those who may move from an area they like for status reasons.[55] Commitment to an area, being a compound of necessity and emotional identification, is not easy to assess and probably requires the use of several subtle techniques. It has been observed that the reasons given for liking a neighborhood tend to be general and abstract, whereas those given for disliking it are more specific and concrete, illustrating the well-known fact that it is easier to know what one does not want than the converse. But it really depends on how carefully one probes into the meaning and intensity of the attitudes expressed. A general question will usually elicit a general, if not also superficial, answer that needs to be supplemented by more specific, detailed probing.

The significance of other residents in determining residential satisfaction emerges whether one asks about reasons for liking or disliking an area. Often, complaints about inadequate dwellings or unsafe streets turn out to be complaints about the habits and standards of neighbors.

In general, then, people are quite favorably disposed toward their residential environments provided these satisfy one or more of their basic value preferences, which vary in content and priority and determine what they are likely to appreciate or criticize most. Surprisingly, perhaps, objective amenities, such as the conditions of dwellings or convenience of transportation, are not of utmost importance to all. The characteristics of other residents, however, seem to be high on everyone's list and contribute to an area's intangible ambiance. These characteristics may determine how people will react to the adequacy of their houses and facilities, whether they intend to stay or move away, and how they cope with noise, overcrowding, and other inconveniences.[56]

In an unusually detailed study of middle class families in two southern cities in the United States, these matters were explored with exceptional skill and care as is evident from the following selective summary of the study's findings.[57] To assess the relative salience of different elements of neighborhood satisfaction, Wilson asked the respondents to choose among alternatives of the following sort: If you could live in "a very good neighborhood but located so that it would be difficult for you to travel to other parts of town or a less desirable neighborhood but located so that it would be easy for you to travel to other parts of town," which would you choose? The respondents favored the good but relatively inaccessible neighborhood 3 to 1. Similarly, a less desirable house in a good neighborhood was preferred 6 to 1 over a good house in a less desirable neighborhood. What did they have in mind when they thought of a "good" neighborhood? The nature of the people living there figured prominently in both sets of responses, followed by the location of stores, schools, churches, and bus lines and a respect for privacy. The relative rank order of the qualities most valued in a neighborhood by one of the samples was: spaciousness (most valued), beauty, good for children, exclusiveness, countrylike, privacy, greenery, homeyness, quietness, cleanliness, newness, friendliness crowdedness, dirtiness (least valued). The respondents also indicated the following qualities as those that they most missed in their current neighborhoods: beauty, exclusiveness, a countrylike character, and spaciousness. The importance of beauty, privacy, and quiet calls for imaginative design quite as much as for appealing social arrangements.

Finally, individuals were shown a list of seventeen facilities and asked to choose those that they most wanted in their "neighborhood" (this was not specified further) and how many of them that they wanted close to home (within a twenty-minute walk). The seven facilities considered most important by respondents in both cities, though with a slightly different rank order, were: an elementary school, grocery store, shopping center, bus stop, religious building, and drugstore. The five items considered least important in a neighborhood were such recreational facilities as a movie theater and a swimming pool and such educational facilities as nurseries and preschool play space. The pattern discovered for these family- and home-centered individuals may not, of course, apply to other types who should also be studied in the same intensive manner.

The overall qualities of neighborhood are the most difficult to assess, and yet they often decisively affect people's reactions. Sometimes these qualities have historical significance, as in the Shitamachi and Yamanote districts of modern Tokyo,[58] or they may reflect current status designations such as gold coasts, slums, and bohemias. These overriding qualities are particularly inaccessible to those unfamiliar with an area or district, and they are not always, or even generally, associated with objective adequacies or inadequacies. Planners may be especially interested in the fact that some of the elements they themselves consider to contribute most to an area's desirability may not turn out to do so in fact. Meyerson has written:

There is a city in the United States that violates most of the first principles of sound urban planning. Its land use is chaotic; its streets come in patches of gridiron fitted neither to themselves nor to their topography; its "in-town" houses are usually made of wood frame and are three-or-four story walkups. Yet it is considered here and abroad one of the most attractive cities in the world. It is, of course, San Francisco.[59]

FACTORS ASSOCIATED WITH LIKING AND DISLIKING NEIGHBORHOOD AREAS ▪

Some areas may exhibit less neighborhood satisfaction than others, not because they are objectively less satis-

factory but because they have a higher concentration of
residents predisposed to being critical and fault-finding
—principally as a prelude to their moving away from
the area. Such individuals, whom Mogey calls "status-
dissenting," constantly try to exercise some personal influence over their environments, and they are thus more
likely to be recent migrants in any setting, since the
process of moving from a familiar to an unfamiliar environment stimulates one's critical faculties.[60] Thus, reactions to the environment are one aspect of a general
outlook on life. And just as people may stay in poor
surroundings because they believe that the future will
be better, so people may abandon superior environments
because these do not meet their tacit status needs.

As the following examples indicate, status aspirations
along with family size, age, and other personal characteristics are important correlates of neighborhood satisfaction.

Higher socioeconomic status tends to be associated
with neighborhood satisfaction and a disinclination to
move out of an area.[61] This reflects both the superiority
of facilities and services such areas provide and an actual or imputed likemindedness among their inhabitants. It seems that satisfied residents perceive greater social similarities between themselves and their neighbors
than may actually exist. Conversely, dissatisfied residents tend to perceive social differences even where
these are minimal. The mechanism of projection that is
operative here must thus be taken into account when
trying to interpret the reasons for failures and successes
in physically planned environments.

In addition to social status factors, neighborhood satisfaction, as revealed in the intention to move, is also

closely tied to the phase of a family's life cycle. Young couples with small children are most eager to move in search of more space.[62] Their decision to move is not unrelated to their ambitions, however, for while the lack of space may be the primary determinant, unsatisfied status needs may give an added impetus.

Finally, length of residence and age of resident strengthen attachment to an area. Older, long-term residents express more neighborhood satisfaction than do younger and newer residents.[63] In the uprootings occasioned by urban renewal, it is especially the aged who suffer from the disruption of ties to local churches, doctors, grocery shops, and clubs (though not always to other residents).[64] Of course, this is linked to the availability of actual or perceived alternatives. Where these are few, people may say that they are satisfied in their present surroundings, but they may be among the first to move once a realistic opportunity presents itself. For this reason it is difficult to predict residential turnover solely on the basis of current attitudes.

In view of the importance of the social characteristics of neighbors in the positive assessments of neighborhoods, physical improvements in housing and services may not achieve the effects desired or assumed by those who stress their priority. Even where the dwelling is of first importance, "isolated houses of desirable quality would not in themselves hold and attract" people.[65] The reputation of an area is often determined by its social rather than its physical climate.

In sum, neither subjectively identified boundaries, nor concentrated use of area facilities, nor neighborly relations, nor sentiments permit us to locate and classify distinctive urban neighborhoods. Today, neighborhoods so identified are either so poor or so wealthy as to be relatively isolated from the mainstream of urban life. The lack of overlap between neighboring, use of facilities, and sentimental attachments means that these cannot be used as indexes for consistently subdividing a larger urban area satisfactorily from both the physical and the social points of view.

On the basis of the admittedly sparse data on how people use given local areas, where they draw boundary lines, and whether they are attached to a local area, we can only conclude, while pleading for more and more systematic data, that the local area is no longer of primary importance. With the exception of grocery stores and perhaps of primary schools, there are very few facilities that must be located near homes for everyone. And as for neighborhood attachments, some urban residents are strongly involved, others only minimally. At best, this is a subjective phenomenon greatly dependent on perceived and actual alternatives to friends, facilities, and dependency on a wider urban area. The economically better off are generally more mobile and less tied to their neighborhoods than the poorer urban residents. Expanded or narrow local horizons seem very much dependent on opportunities for mobility and on personal selectivity. Although physical neighborhoods may still be identified, their leading positions as providers of information, identity, and social relations have been displaced by social change in the family, work, and mass entertainment and amusement.

Concentration on the local area, no matter how imprecisely defined, seems to be most strongly correlated with a lack of alternatives. This applies, for example, when town centers are too distant, their facilities too

costly, or not appealing due to unfamiliarity or ignorance. It also applies when isolation is due either to
local self-sufficiency or to strong ideological and social
pressures. That is, where a solidary local network of
close economic, cultural, social, and physical ties already
exists, there local loyalties and activities will be strong.
This does not, however, mean that the provision of local
services will by themselves stimulate the desired local
loyalties and sentiments in areas lacking the social and
historic preconditions for such solidarity.

Today, it seems that local self-sufficiency and self-
reliance are diminishing everywhere. Even remote villages are linked to the urban-industrial world via mass
transport and mass media of communication, local
branches of national associations, and personal use of
urban centers for amusement or learning. The utility of
the neighborhood conception has in consequence been
reexamined by many planners who increasingly find it
wanting. Before discussing the implications of the sociological evidence here reviewed, a brief summary of the
main conclusions is in order.

CONCLUSION ■

Two main questions have guided this inquiry:

1. According to existing evidence, how much and what
   kinds of neighboring occur in different types of settlements and what factors account for the patterns
   found?
2. What is the evidence for the existence of neighborhoods in modern urban settings?

PATTERNS OF NEIGHBORING ■

To answer the first question we had to consider the varying definitions of the role of neighbor, for this role determines the meaning of manifest neighboring activities. Despite wide variations in practice, in principle this role assigns to neighbors a place intermediate between friends and relatives as regards their duties toward and feelings about one another. Neighbors are expected to assist each other during emergencies, to be sociable in a delimited way, and to do their part in maintaining common standards of conduct and physical upkeep in a given space.

Neighboring activities, diffuse and difficult to grasp in their complex entirety, may be analyzed according to several different dimensions, each capable of independent variation. These dimensions include the frequency of neighboring, its priority, intensity, extent, formality, locale, and occasion. These were found to vary by setting, by group and class affiliations, and by personal inclinations. Neighboring activities and relationships are more fully integrated with social and economic life in small towns and villages or in special cultural and occupational enclaves in cities than in big urban centers, where friends tend to replace neighbors as sources of assistance and sociability. As individuals and groups become more self-sufficient and as the capacity of local institutions to meet current crises wanes, the need for neighborly assistance diminishes. Fewer crises, more alternatives for dealing with them, increasing individuality and selectivity, and more mobility and fluidity, all make neighboring less compulsory and more variable.

Traditions of place and of social class seem to exert a

general determinative influence on patterns of neighboring within which personal characteristics and physical design play their particular parts. The rise of new values and institutions, the shift from an extended to a conjugal, companionate, family system, and the availability of alternative sources of amusement and employment also change the content and meaning of neighboring. It is not so much a decline in interpersonal neighboring that we observe as a chance in the organization of life itself accompanied by new values, priorities, and preferences.

Neighboring in dynamic urban areas is no longer part of a tight network of interdependent activities and obligations concentrated within a small physical and social space; it is simply one more segmentalized activity. Only the most isolated, poorest, most immobile segments of the population continue to rely on the local area and its inhabitants—though not even they do so exclusively, taking for granted a degree of choice and change that would have been inconceivable in a less dynamic era.

The consequences of spatial mobility on neighboring have often been observed though not always correctly assessed. The immediate rise in observed sociability following a move to certain suburbs or housing estates led to certain hasty and premature conclusions about the favorable effects of suburbs or better houses as such. Such increased sociability among newcomers does accompany the early period of adjustment to a strange environment, but it is by no means a permanent feature of their lives. Neighbors do turn to one another for assistance and fellowship during this period of stress and strangeness, which is difficult for all, but once things are back to normal individuals become more selective in their neighboring and specialized in their interests. This is true both for working class and middle class groups, for individuals who came from solidary areas high in traditional neighboring as well as for those moving from areas where more segmentalized neighbor relations prevailed.

In all of this, age, personal temperament, and individual taste must be considered as secondary factors. It is true that children and adolescents may neighbor more or nearer to their homes or that extroverts may do so more than introverts, but these facts cannot be considered apart from the broader context shaped by social traditions and the dynamics of social change. Nor can design as such be said to determine the use of physical space in and around dwellings. Under certain social conditions of perceived or actual like-mindedness, common footpaths, utilities, or landings may help promote pleasant social encounters. But if these common facilities are to be shared by mutually antagonistic groups, then the common footpaths may well turn into warpaths. The mixing of different social groups is a complex and delicate matter requiring skills not yet delineated in any existing formula.

EXISTENCE OF NEIGHBORHOODS ■

A number of unsolved problems are found when we consider the existence of neighborhoods. Using the presence of boundaries or the use of local facilities as indicators works very well where these two—boundary and functioning neighborhood—are in fact joined, each being an expression of the existence of the other. A problem arises when we try to employ these indicators as independent measures, as "proof" of the presence of neighborhoods or, worse, when we try to use them as promoters of neighborhood formation—in this case generally, and perhaps necessarily, we fail. It appears that such phenomena as clear-cut boundaries, concentrated use of local facilities, and strong local loyalties are only the expressions of neighborhood cohesion—not their causes. By identifying physical boundaries, therefore, we have not taken more than a faltering first step in location of neighborhoods, even though most functioning neighborhoods usually have either natural or man-made boundaries.

Moreover, the very same forces that have altered and in part eroded neighboring activities and relations have also been at work on neighborhoods. "Where one resides," Reginald Isaacs once wrote, "is not necessarily where one lives."[66] This is by and large true not merely for the small town, but it is also increasingly true for urban aggregates in general. Usually, those neighborhoods that are in fact neighborhoods in the traditional sense (that is, clearly marked by physical and social boundaries) are also somehow atypical in being isolated or outside the mainstream of urban life—economically, as in extremely wealthy or extremely poor districts; socially, as in slums or suburbs; and culturally, as in racial or immigrant ghettoes. To duplicate only their surface configurations without duplicating the conditions that gave rise to them is as unfeasible as it would be ineffectual.

The boundaries recognized by individuals themselves may facilitate their subjective orientation to their environment. However, such boundaries can hardly serve as an objective demarcation since they are usually much smaller and more variable than the boundaries of political precincts, religious parishes, or planning units. Moreover, there is as yet no evidence that these subjective boundaries coincide either with special attachments to or concentrated use of local areas.

Nor is satisfaction with one's local area a better criterion for identifying the existence of separate neighborhoods. People are hesitant to admit dissatisfactions or to find fault with their particular neighborhoods, and only careful and explicit probing can uncover more meaningful discriminations. Paradoxically, it is not difficult to obtain complaints from people about their neighborhoods. They will readily catalogue the negative features of their neighborhoods but will not alter their overall favorable assessments of them. The whole problem of the relation between subjective judgments and objective inadequacies of neighborhoods has been all too little explored. People may be greatly attached to their neighborhoods and yet leave them. The young and ambitious, the highly status-conscious, and certain personality types are generally more critical and more mobile irrespective of the objective characteristics of their environment. But even older, more stable, settled residents may not hesitate to move from neighborhoods that they like in order to take advantages of better opportunities elsewhere. Thus, liking an area—at least in urban areas—is not necessarily indicative of establishing permanent roots there.

Local attachments are, of course, greater among long-term residents of a neighborhood, among "block" rather than "city" dwellers as one classification would have it, and among those satisfied with or resigned to their current social status. But in a dynamic urban setting, these groups, no matter how empirically prevalent, do not typify the inherent tendencies of the urban-industrial age with its pressures for movement and variety. This does not, of course, imply that their particular needs and problems should be ignored or overlooked but rather that they be considered in perspective. The dynamic forces of urban-industrial society are not concentrated in these groups or realized through them, since isolation and immobility are, perhaps unjustly, considered peculiar anachronisms or undesirable, and if possible temporary, marks of deprivation.

More typical of the realities of this century are those individuals and families seeking more space, better jobs, higher status, or greater amenities. For these people local areas or neighborhoods are but stepping-stones— not necessarily devoid of sentimental value—in the pursuit of happiness. Perhaps future research will tell us that twentieth-century urban man had a utilitarian rather than a sentimental attitude to the areas in which he resided. Perhaps, today, sentiment is itself a specialized emotion attaching itself to selected points in a wider area—to a particular street, or a favorite dwelling, or an ancient monument, but not to the entire subarea in which one happens to live. Like urban man himself, ever in pursuit of actual or imagined opportunities, his emotions and sentiments are not fixed but travel along with him, staying where he stays and moving as he moves, in the varied course of his dynamic life.

This, then, is the weight of the sociological evidence on neighboring. The implications of its message for physical planners will be considered in the final chapters of this book.

3 The Neighborhood Unit Reconsidered

Almost from its inception the "neighborhood unit" idea, inspired by the writings of Ebenezer Howard[1] and first explicitly proposed by Clarence Perry[2] in 1923, has enjoyed wide currency. In essence, this concept refers to a delimited area and population sharing basic facilities and services that are conveniently accessible, on foot, to the individual households. Perry specified the size, boundaries, and street system as among the six basic elements of such a unit and was actually far less dogmatic in his initial proposals than many who followed him.

The concept of a neighborhood unit arose in protest against what the city was doing to man and what man, in turn, was doing to parts of the city. It appealed to diverse groups and individuals including the adherents of the Garden City Movement, social workers coping with settlement house work in slums and immigrant districts, traffic experts,[3] large-scale real estate developers seeking to protect their investments, architects and engineers favoring its economy of design and construction, and moralists and poets at war with "cities where the human heart is sick." In particular, it promised to be an antidote to the monotony and drabness of housing estates built between the two world wars of this century. Breaking up these large areas with their architectural and social uniformity and lack of local color into smaller, more manageable units, would, it was hoped, increase both the efficiency of their operation and local pride and participation in their fate. Specifically, the neighborhood unit was to do the following: (1) introduce a principle of physical order into the chaotic, fragmented urban aggregate; (2) reintroduce local, face-to-face types of contacts into the anonymous urban society, thereby helping to regain some sense of community; (3) encourage the formation of local loyalties and attachments and thereby offset the impact of extensive social and residential mobility; (4) stimulate feelings of identity, security, stability, and rootedness in a world threatening such feelings on all sides; and (5) provide a local training ground for the development of larger loyalties to city and nation.[4]

From the start, therefore, the neighborhood unit was both a social and a planning concept.[5] It also had several, somewhat incompatible, objectives. In one sense, it was to be the "cell" from which the larger city grows and thus be but one link in a complex chain of activities. In another sense, it was to be focused on its own inner resources and central facilities and so develop a distinctive identity as well as partial self-sufficiency in basic facilities, services, and amenities. In yet a third sense, it was to be a service area with shops, open spaces, and social centers, the keynote here being efficiency and utility. In the varied applications of this concept—ranging from the British New Towns, Vallingby (Sweden), Sabende (Guinea) to Sputnik, Moscow, Radburn (New Jersey), and Reston (Virginia)—these different interpretations of the neighborhood unit were not always clearly specified. As a consequence, objective analysis of the validity of the particular interpretation was impeded.

Before we turn to some of the main criticisms of the neighborhood unit, many made by the physical planners themselves, it might be helpful to consider the complicated task of the planners for whom this type of compact formula has its not inconsiderable attractions. Suppose that you were asked to fill in an empty space with people, facilities, houses, roads, and other services, and suppose furthermore that you were to do this under the pressure of time and limited personal and financial resources. Where would you start? Should you consider the area and the needs of its future occupants in their aggregate dimensions or should you resort to some, no matter how tentative, principles of classification that would permit you to subdivide the large "empty" space into more manageable, conceptually graspable units? Clearly, this will in part depend on your assumptions about such subunits and their functions in urban places, which will, in turn, rest on what you know or believe about local loyalties in our urban age. Many planners advocate planned neighborhoods not because they have reliable evidence that this is what urban residents desire or need but because this conforms to certain cherished values that they hope to preserve. Such values, sustained by faith rather than knowledge, are not likely to change in the face of evidence, no matter how persuasive it be. However, there are also those who advocate the utility and desirability of neighborhood units on the grounds that existing evidence supports them. This review of neighborhood units in practice is primarily addressed to thcm.

APPLICATION OF THE NEIGHBORHOOD UNIT IDEA ■

The neighborhood unit idea was first applied in the United States and from there went on to conquer and then partly to lose favor with the planning world. Since Perry's original formulation, in which the role of physical design was much more developed than that of the social aspects, the conception has been modified to take into account varied local conditions as well as the accelerated growth rates of modern cities.

Once the conception gained hold, debate centered mainly on the physical size, the population, the types of facilities and services to be provided, and the relation between the neighborhood unit and the larger community of which it was a part. Even on these points, however, agreement has overshadowed disagreement as planners, rather than have to struggle afresh with each new assignment, sought to convert these tentative general assumptions into practical procedural principles.

The two elements on which planners found themselves most in accord were the small size and relative self-sufficiency of such a unit, modified only by its dependence on a larger urban network. Perry, somewhat reluctantly, had proposed as an optimum unit 5,000 people centered on a primary school of 600 pupils serviced by local shops and a local assembly area within walking distance. Ring roads for vehicular traffic providing both the physical boundary as well as the link to the wider world were to encircle the entire area. Several of these neighborhood units were to comprise a community. Thus, size was to be estimated on the basis of the number of families needed to provide the target number of local primary school pupils; distances were to be determined by the criterion of pedestrian access to all essential facilities; and the number of facilities was to be based on existing standards of residents' needs and desires for shops, churches, movies, parks, and clinics near their homes.[6]

Attempts to test the practical validity of this concept have been hampered by its inconsistent applications; each potential test in a "real life" situation represented a somewhat different version of the concept as originally planned. In the British New Towns, for example, the neighborhood unit had to be accommodated to the smaller-size British primary schools, which meant that no single primary school could become the neighborhood core. Also, the number of shops actually servicing the New Town populations fell far short of the plan, whether for financial reasons or special population characteristics is not yet clear.[7] Cinemas, having been displaced by television, can no longer be regarded as essential for each neighborhood unit, and other amenities such as branch libraries and youth and community centers either failed to be established or were too sparsely distributed. In Korangi, Pakistan, to take another example, the absence of certain higher order facilities such as schools and markets likewise altered the plan, thereby precluding a genuine assessment of its actual operation.[8] These practical deviations from the original plan make a full test of the concept difficult; however, they do permit a piecemeal testing of some of its elements.[9]

According to Nicholson, no aspect of life in the British New Towns is more difficult to assess than the neighborhood unit, nor are its presumed advantages everywhere automatically apparent. Subunits for daily shopping and primary schooling may be clearly indicated, and some buffer between individuals and central authorities is also useful. However, the problems of economic duplication of services and thus of competition between neighborhood and town centers and of a division of loyalties between the neighborhood and the town have not as yet been resolved. If people concentrate spiritually, socially, and economically on a neighborhood area, the town as a whole will be deprived of their participation and patronage; whereas if they ignore the neighborhood and concentrate on the town, then the neighborhood unit is clearly superfluous.

In addition to these important practical observations, certain of the concept's fundamental assumptions about human behavior have been challenged in recent years. Increasingly, for example, planners have become less dogmatic about the ideal size of such local units. The pace of population growth as well as revolutionary developments in transportation and communication facilities have forced them to think in terms of larger, more complex sectors. Perry's original target size of 5,000 is considered by some to be too large for genuine neighboring. They assert that it is both insufficiently intimate and insufficiently urban.[10] Experience has shown that if a neighborhood center is to provide a range of standard urban services it needs from three to four times as many consumers as originally stipulated. This would call for two types of local units, a smaller and a larger one, each performing different functions. The larger one would provide basic amenities for somewhere around 20,000 people; the smaller one, whose size remains problematical, would encourage social intimacy.

Planners also hesitate to make the nucleus of neighborhood life a single institution such as a primary school. Just as it is unwise to plan a national economy around a single product so it is unwise to make a single activity the hub of local life. Experience from Sweden and the Soviet Union has indicated that in a changing society a change in the educational system entails a reorganization of all local units whose physical configuration depends on it.[11]

Another basic criticism concerns the undesirable consequences of social segregation stemming from the focus of the neighborhood unit on young families with young children. To make the primary school a nucleus of local life for adults without children or for unmarried individuals is patently absurd. However, in Perry's and his followers' schemes one looks in vain for a consideration of the needs of these groups. Not only do we find an overemphasis on young families with small children, but also within this category the neighborhood unit favors those families valuing the things such units can provide—namely, intimacy, quiet, green spaces, playgrounds for the children, and pedestrian access to primary services. In addition, their economic similarities further promote a leveling of means and taste in the services desired. In most new towns there is, in fact, an extremely high degree of segregation by income as well as by family composition. Most of the new town residents inhabit standard rent housing; any nonstandard houses tend to be concentrated in one or two neighborhood units so that no balance of social classes is created within these units.[12] Those who consider the mixing of diverse social groups as either undesirable or unfeasible are neither surprised nor dismayed by these findings, but those who see the neighborhood as a miniature of the larger world, as a cornerstone for a more complex, urban existence are disturbed by the failure of neighborhood units to achieve some sort of social balance.

This leads to a final, highly controversial point of criticism concerning the significance of the local area in an urbanized, megalopolitan world. Designing self-contained, or at least self-absorbed, neighborhood units, it is argued, deprives people of some notable advantages of urban life. Some individuals and groups may indeed welcome the intimate small town atmosphere and face-to-face contacts such units intend to foster, but others, truer to the urban ethos, prefer to use the whole city and to travel to their social contacts or work. As we have seen, neighboring, the use of local facilities, and attachment to local areas are highly variable in modern cities, depending on group and class traditions, on general levels of life, and on personal inclination. If this is the case, then how can one expect the neighborhood unit to succeed in all settings? Its utility for certain groups such as the more isolated or immobile may be undeniable, but even here no overall formula is needed.

This is where the incompatibility of the several goals of the neighborhood unit referred to earlier emerges in full force. From its inception the neighborhood unit carried a double burden, which may help account for its erratic performance in practice. On the one hand, it was to provide convenience and comfort and direct, face-to-face contacts in order to restore some sense of community that had been disturbed or destroyed by the specialization and segmentalization of urban life. On the other hand, however, it was also to constitute a special subpart of a larger, more complex totality. In the first case it was to be a somewhat self-contained, personal, "little community." In the second sense it was to be but a specialized fragment of a wider domain, which could not constitute a world for its members, but merely act as one of the means, an instrumentality, for the attainment of larger goals and purposes. Residents are thus under dual, somewhat incompatible pressures, and they may, not surprisingly, develop confused and inconsistent beliefs and conceptions about the significance of their neighborhoods vis á vis the city as a whole. As a result of the misgivings and doubts raised by these criticisms, a number of planners and other specialists have proposed alternatives to the neighborhood unit that modify the original concept in significant ways.

ALTERNATIVE PROPOSALS ▪

Not everyone agrees that the principle of the neighborhood unit should be completely abandoned. Some feel that it has never been given a proper chance either because of inadequacies in its design[13] or its application. They urge a proper, full-scale test before the concept is rejected as unworkable, a test that would permit us to specify the reasons for its failure or success under given conditions.[14] In reply one might argue that the reasons for the inconsistent and partial application of the concept may themselves be indirect proof of its conceptual inadequacies. The very need for flexibility to accommodate the variety of needs and demands of a heterogeneous population implies that no single formula may be workable. This rather than a lack of funds or unimaginative design may be at the root of the problem.

A number of planners and social scientists have come to favor alternatives which would not reject the concept *in toto* but modify it by incorporating research findings on patterns of neighboring and the use of local facilities and services by an urban-industrial population. Among these are the neighborhood circle, the social network, and the roving neighborhood.

PERSONAL AND IMPERSONAL UNITS ■

The absence of formal constraints on neighboring relationships in urban areas permits individual predispositions and desires to come to the fore. As a result, the boundaries of an individual's choices follow no set or predictable pattern. Some urban residents have extensive ties with other residents, others have few, some go far afield, while others confine their contacts near home. Accordingly, some planners have incorporated these social research findings into their planning schemes by proposing a division of the neighborhood unit into a smaller, personal neighboring circle or network and a larger, impersonal service area. The neighboring circle may include all relatives and acquaintances within a given area, all known by sight, greeted, or chatted with, or only those with whom more intimate contacts are maintained. Studies have found the number of such contacts to vary considerably. In Hamburg, for example, such a circle included up to forty families from houses adjacent to or opposite one's own. Beyond a certain point on that street people were no longer certain whether to greet each other or not. In a well-to-do area of private villas, such uncertainty began with the third house on either side.[15] Bott likewise considers the "social network" to be the significant "immediate social environment of urban families," which, depending on the social similarities among the residents, may be confined to or transcend local area boundaries.[16] Naturally, the shapes of the boundaries established in this subjective fashion will vary as the propensity to neighboring among the inhabitants varies.

Jacqueline Tyrrwhitt, an early advocate of the two-fold local unit, suggests the terms "social unit," to consist of about 500 households, or 2,000 persons, within which social contacts between like-minded individuals could unfold, and "urban unit," to designate a much larger area containing from 30,000 to 70,000 people and providing a wide variety of modern urban facilities and services.[17] These suggestions have been taken one step further by Kuper, who links them to his distinction between "reserved" and "sociable" neighbors, suggesting that the service unit is better suited to the reserved type resident and the neighborly unit to the sociable type [18]

Kuper, along with others, sees an inherent incompatibility between these two types of units. If planners construct a neighborhood unit on the principle of personal, face to face relations, he argues, they are bound to weaken the service unit.

The very circumstances that favour the service unit are believed to defeat the objective of promoting communities. . . . The smaller the group, the more difficult it is to provide for relative self-sufficiency and the greater the pull to other areas. The larger the group, the more readily may activities of residents be contained within the area, but at the same time, the smaller the likelihood of social relationships ramifying through the neighbourhood.[19]

Here we are again reminded of the inverse relationship between the need for and reliance on neighbors and the availability of public services and facilities.

Some would ignore the personal neighboring unit altogether and concentrate entirely on the planning of larger, impersonal areas for shopping, health, culture, and recreation. In fact, Mann observes that since neither the establishment of a community center as a focal point of neighborhood life nor the social mixing of various groups for the sake of social balance has been realized by means of neighborhood units as originally formulated, what remains of the original conception is essentially the idea of "the neighbourhood as an amenity area with shops, schools, institutions, open spaces, and road patterns laid down in accordance with a thought-out plan." [20] Many feel that it is only or primarily in this sense that the neighborhood unit "has fully justified itself." Glikson goes so far as to suggest that without some such concept the proper allocation of public amenities and services is virtually impossible.[21]

Planning for amenity areas rather than for neighborhood units in the traditional sense means that planners will continue to search for ways to subdivide a territory into small, more manageable subunits, but they will not expect these to promote primary social relationships. It also means that the use of facilities and services offered in such units need not be confined to residents living in the immediate vicinity. Amenity areas might, therefore, be designed on a numerical and geographical basis with only minimum attention being paid to the social and cultural characteristics of local inhabitants. The services of these areas would draw on users from a variety of points in the urban complex.

In this connection, however, the unavoidable social reality of class and ethnic subdivisions with their impact on tastes and financial resources cannot be ignored. If such realities are not taken into account, the division of an urban area into numerically equal subunits with identical facilities and services may be wasteful and ineffectual. One way to cope with this problem is for planners to concentrate on minimum facilities, such as shops, clinics, and transportation stops, which are not deeply influenced by the social and cultural characteristics of a population. Of course, even here it matters whether the residents are wealthy enough to afford cars and vacations or are tied to mass transport or to recreation near at hand. If it is true that people of "different sexes, ages, and different social classes have different types of interests and different physical areas within which interests are pursued," then any mechanical subdivision according to distance, numbers, or densities is bound to be inappropriate.[22]

Whatever the final resolution of these questions, it is apparent that the neighborhood unit—in its original, inclusive sense—is not in these changing times a useful one. For this reason, perhaps, such units that "formed an essential part of many town development plans have tended to fall into disrepute or be relegated to the status of convenient administrative and service machinery." [23] In some of the more recent British New Towns the concept has been dispensed with altogether. For example, Hook, the town that was never built, had plans to preserve only some of the technical features of the unit concept. The plans provided for the segregation of pedestrian from vehicular traffic and the distribution of primary schools. Similarly, Cumbernauld strove to create a more compact and urban town by doubling densities, by carefully planning vehicular and pedestrian traffic networks, and by making the single town center easily accessible. Its success in achieving its aims must await the completion of the town center along with the attainment of the target population. Some would argue that the retention of such principles or features as the allocation of primary schools on a residential basis and of pedestrian accessibility has only modified but not displaced the neighborhood unit concept. This argument ignores the main innovation of these plans, which was to do away with the idea of identical subunits bearing a uniform residential stamp by explicitly recognizing that "a more mobile community in the motor age makes it fruitless to search for a universal formula." [24]

THE "ROVING NEIGHBORHOOD" ■

In addition to a personal neighborhood circle, Riemer proposes the "roving neighborhood." [25] He notes that in between large areas that follow the rapid transit lines and divide a city into west, east, north, and south (and are usually devoid of any precise social meaning) and the smaller more intimate area of residential contacts, there develops a sense of identification with some sort of "roving" neighborhood that may be centered around points of interest other than individual residences, such as the local high school or the shopping district. A given individual may belong to several such roving neighborhoods at the same time, with each service focus having its own radius of users. These service radii, sometimes delineated by natural or man-made barriers, may be separate or overlapping. Only if "the service radius happens to coincide for several such facilities, will it be advantageous to integrate them into a unified plan." But to insist in advance that "such integration will have to be related to the walking distance neighborhood" strikes Riemer as an unwarranted assumption.[26] The size of such a service radius will then not be some magic number of 5,000 or 10,000 but will depend on the nature of the shared activities and on their tendency toward clustering or toward dispersion.

Noting that the heterogeneity of cities works against the pedestrian scale in local areas (for example, when church membership must transcend local spatial boundaries to achieve a certain size), Riemer would add five types of "walking distance areas" to supplement these service radii. These areas, based on the most frequent activity around which other contact points are clustered, include the residential, occupational, educational, commercial, and associational walking distance area. The residential walking distance area is thus considered to be only one among several types suited to special groups, such as the very young and their caretakers, the very old, and recent immigrants without means. The other walking distance areas would be focused on other service radii, for example, a drugstore located close to a college or medical services close to places of employment.[27]

A similar notion is contained in the concept of *regroupement intermediaires*. This favors the planning of

activities around transportation stops, restaurants near
places of employment, cafes, cinemas, or hairdressers,
wherever, that is, the same people regularly encounter
one another during certain hours, days, or weeks for activities which are habitual rather than communal.[28]

THE "SERVICE NEIGHBORHOOD" ■

The idea of roving neighborhoods is interesting but
difficult to translate into planning practice. Certainly it
cannot be put into effect without some concept of a
hierarchy of services similar to that proposed by Doxiadis, or earlier, by the MARS group.[29] In these proposals, a large urban area is subdivided into a series of interlocking service areas going from the most inclusive and
complex unit, where activities are highly concentrated,
to less complex and also smaller ones containing more
frequently used or more basic facilities. These units, organized into layers or levels, range from the lowest level
comprising a few families on a single street to the highest level servicing more than a half a million people and
embracing the entire metropolitan area. In addition to
varying by size, population, and principal mode of
transport employed, each hierarchical level varies also
according to the nature, size, and scope of its center.
The advantages of a service hierarchy are its flexibility
and the avoidance of monotony by distributing activities, functions, and services in a series of overlapping
circles more truly reflective of the urban pattern. Each
resident, moreover, does not belong more fully to one
subunit—such as the residential one—than to others.
His participation is geared to some principle of needs
and priorities on which the whole hierarchy is based.

The problem with current versions of service hierarchies concerns the cutting points between levels. Most of these are too empirical. They are based, for example, on how many people are needed to support a wholesale market, flower shops, or an opera house; or they may be based on how many frequent health clinics, universities, or specialty markets, which is bound to vary from place to place according to economic resources and customs. The cut-off points between levels are also arbitrary divisions reflecting personal assumptions about the ways in which people should be using various facilities, how often, and at what distances. As a preliminary tool, such a hierarchy is useful provided it is continually revised as more information on human needs and patterns of movement within cities is made available.

THE NEIGHBORHOOD OF "COLLECTIVE RESPONSIBILITY" ▪

A final alternative is based on insights gained from community organization and action programs. Realizing that the mobility and heterogeneity of urban life have undermined the more traditional forces of social cohesion required for a pooling of collective resources in the solution of common problems, some architects would recommend designs that give local units a collective framework by encouraging local leadership. If local areas were to assume such collective responsibilities as fire and police protection, property maintenance, and recreation, as they did in preindustrial cities, local loyalties and commitments may once again be revived. In the absence of such common undertakings, informal social bonds, even where present, are neither sufficiently stable nor enduring enough to promote local community life. In fact, it has been said that to make personal, variable needs and sentiments bear the burden of creating rather than of merely giving expression to internal moral and emotional cohesion is to take the ephemeral for the substance, to "bind together without a king-pin." [30] Formal organization and local leadership are thus seen as antidotes to urban drift and rootlessness.

This view corresponds on the local scene to major trends in the larger society where formal organizations are likewise designed to promote the continuity and coherence not provided by shifting populations of temporary neighbors, strangers, isolates, and reserved urbanites. The introduction of formally organized, locally based leaders forming the nucleus for sustained local activities and projects encourages and sustains a neighborhood spirit and identity despite rapid rates of residential turnover and the absence of strong bonds of sentiment or tradition among residents.

These neighborhood programs are largely an outgrowth of the urban research carried on at the University of Chicago in the early decades of this century, culminating in what has come to be known as the "Chicago School." This work showed that a number of social phenomena were associated with so-called "natural areas," areas having both an ecological and a cultural relation to the rest of the city. The highest rates of delinquency, for example, were concentrated in certain poor, transitional, immigrant zones succumbing to the pressures of a rapidly growing city. The interesting fact about these points of concentration, however, was that the delinquency patterns did not characterize the residents apart from the area. As the older ethnic immigrant groups moved away in their pursuit of the American Dream, the percentage of juvenile delinquents stayed constant in the areas that they abandoned to new and different groups. In the areas to which these groups moved there was a decrease in the delinquency rates. The high rates of delinquency were thus area-bound. This led the original researchers to conclude that the persistence of high delinquency rates in particular areas of the city was due to social disorganization— in particular, to the absence of organized collective efforts to ameliorate local conditions. Their solution was to propose a "program of physical rehabilitation of slum areas and the development of community organization" consisting of a "group of leading citizens of a neighborhood who take the responsibility of a program for delinquency treatment and prevention." [31] Accordingly, they encouraged the establishment of neighborhood discussion and action groups, patterned on the New England Town Meetings, for the purposes of neighborhood improvements. These organizations, patterned along ethnic lines, were at best only moderately successful and died out as their members became absorbed in the mainstream of American political and cultural life.

Similar attempts have been tried since the thirties with equally mixed results. A particularly successful experiment is the "Back of the Yards" rehabilitation effort, organized along the ideas of Saul Alinsky, in a notorious Chicago slum. In this four-square-mile area of more than 100,000 second- and third-generation inhabitants of European Catholic immigrant stock, a physical and economic rebirth followed its organizing along these lines. Preceded by a fifteen-year program of short-range improvement efforts, the large-scale rehabilitation effort succeeded in part because, according to Alinsky, a well-staffed, well-financed community organization gradually took root. It developed into a major power structure and an articulate spokesman for the area in the city government. But while the program increased the self-confidence of the residents by making them more articulate and aware of legal, educational, and health needs and resources, it did not, apparently, decrease crime and delinquency rates. Whatever else its problems, moreover, the area may have derived some advantage from its high proportion of home owners and low rate of residential turnover.[32] One wonders whether such a program would be equally successful under the more typical urban conditions of high residential turnover and the propensity among urban dwellers to rent rather than to own their homes. Such factors, which may be a spur to the initiative and cooperation demanded by such self-help programs, may be crucial variables affecting their outcome. Predictably, traditional neighborhoods with a well-established cultural and social identity would seem to have an advantage under these conditions.

Jane Jacobs also considers self-management necessary for a successful city neighborhood. It should operate at two levels—the street and the district. The street neighborhoods are essentially those where the routine of daily life goes on—meetings, shopping, and just strolling. The vitality, concerns, needs, and interests of residents are expressed there. On the district level the more impersonal, organizational forces of the city become decisive. Jacobs sees these districts, represented by effective leaders or spokesmen, as intermediaries between the powerful city and the powerless street. She correctly observes that self-management means different things at different levels. At the street level it involves resident participation, active concern for common local problems, and a network of interdependent human relationships that give color and meaning to local life. At the district level the ability to formulate broad policies, to relate to the city as a whole, and to deal with city hall directly to obtain necessary public improvements and services becomes crucial. Street and district thus have distinctive, yet equally essential, organizational objectives—one stresses the unique personal character of the local habitat, the other forms a common link to a wider external world on which the local unit depends.[33]

THE ROLE OF THE PHYSICAL PLANNER ▪

What, then, can we say about the role of physical planning in helping to create a sense of community? As a number of studies of newly planned towns and neighborhoods have shown, social solidarity and cooperation are less responsive to physical layout and design than planners would wish. There is considerable reason to doubt that these can, by themselves, either promote or inhibit neighborhood loyalty and sociability. Existing evidence suggests that where residents share certain basic attitudes and ambitions (and these vary by culture and social class), physical features may facilitate social encounters (though not necessarily more intimate personal relationships), but only under rare and unusual circumstances will they also promote an active, purposive community life. In fact, one is tempted to conclude that only where the preconditions are favorable for such a community, can physical design and siting play its intended role at all. Social class and status differences can disrupt the most compact physical arrangements, and the boundaries of gossip chains and other informal social networks do not necessarily, or even usually, conform to the planners' designated boundaries. In conjunction with other factors, most of these yet to be established by careful research, physical and spatial design may contribute to but not determine social interaction. The role of such design is auxiliary rather than autonomous. As we have seen, without acceptable and accepted leaders, common projects, or perceived bonds of interest, utility, or affection, the physically contiguous cannot, apparently, also become socially united.

CONCLUSION ■

Both partisans and critics of the neighborhood unit concept find its main utility as a service area. It provides a link between territorially bound activities related to work, residence, schooling, or recreation and activities encompassing the whole, complex, and far-flung urban network. Only where local areas are also isolated geographically or culturally can the neighborhood unit assume the social significance originally anticipated. But more and more, local areas are losing their autonomy. They are being increasingly drawn in, and thus defined, by the shape and structure of the larger urban framework to which they belong. Their erstwhile autonomy is perhaps still visible in the more deprived areas of cities, areas cut off from the main currents of economic opportunity and cultural variety. Thus their autonomy is in part an index of their deprivation. While this "autonomy" may strengthen the social solidarity and identity of the inhabitants, it does not add to their collective standing in the wider city. Here, other factors come into play, significantly the impression an area makes on the citizens and its reputation as relatively desirable or undesirable in light of some broader yardstick of values. In this sense the totality serves as a frame of reference for the locality.

Today this totality is increasingly characterized by mobility, dispersion, and heterogeneity, which work against a concentration of activities and sentiments in local areas and hence of the integration of men within such areas. In an era in which the mainsprings of industrial life are found in the teeming metropolitan centers it is these centers that compel and attract attention. To them come the young, the inquisitive, the ambitious, and the deviants, all seeking anonymity, opportunity, and an enlarged arena for their activities and dreams. Short of transferring the dynamic qualities of the metropolitan area to the local scene, which would mean nothing less than transforming it into an urban complex, one can hardly expect the inhabitants to confine their field of vision to the local unit. The ubiquitousness of change, the fluidity of men in urban places, the search for pleasure and comfort in urban, often anonymous, settings, all have their roots not in the peculiar mentality of a marginal minority but in the conditions of life of the growing majority. These conditions do not make the walking-distance neighborhood the preferred spatial arrangement for all types of urbanites.

In the following chapter the chief findings of our review will be summarized and scrutinized for their possible implications for physical planning.

4 Implications for Planning the Human Environment

If the suggestions developed in this review of sociologically relevant findings on patterns of neighboring are to be used by planners in their work, it is necessary to consider the broader implications. It is one thing to say that planners must be sensitive to the social and personal characteristics of their clients and another to show what difference this sensitivity would make in their actual planning of projects. When planners start on a project, they can hardly afford the luxury of either doing surveys on local characteristics and attitudes or waiting for the results of such exhaustive surveys. In order that planners have such information available on which to base their decisions, it is suggested that there be a division of labor within the planning profession between those specializing in the translation of evidence from auxiliary disciplines into practical planning measures and those devoted to carrying on the day-to-day routines. There is probably always some time lag between the discovery of new knowledge and its application. Hopefully, however, methods may be developed to incorporate such knowledge in the ongoing planning process. Practitioners may not be able to stop and wait for confirmed evidence, but they can be made increasingly aware of the shifting balance between knowledge and speculation, faith and fact so that today's inadequate yardsticks, used for want of something better, are not viewed as rigid formulas but as flexible and changing principles.

Flexibility to changing times and circumstances is one problem. Sensitivity to changing scales is another. Much of the evidence reviewed concerns generalizations about small numbers of people, but in large parts of the world today the planners' task is to design space and facilities for large population aggregates, many of them poor, inarticulate, and unsettled in their ways of life. How can one bridge these two? Here again, a division of labor might be in order between those expert in macro- and in micro-scale planning. There is probably some relation between the two types of planning, but their joint and separate characteristics have not been sufficiently clarified.

Finally, there is the knotty question of how to plan for a changing population, a point we stressed in discussing the phases of neighboring under different conditions and at different time periods in a settlement's life. Here the implications are clear. In addition to keeping an ongoing record of the impact of these changes on people's relations to space and to each other, planners may find it advisable to classify facilities and services into primary and secondary types. The primary types—such as shopping, church going, schooling, and transportation—may be considered so general and universal that broad, widely agreed upon principles concerning them may well emerge. The secondary types such as cultural and recreational facilities, are more variable and changing. It may not be possible to plan for them in a general way at all. Since we know, for example, that certain types of low income groups tend to be more bound to local areas than others, we would plan their facilities accordingly. Since we also know, however, that as their standards of living rise so does their mobility, we would need to plan these basic facilities for alternative uses or for alternative populations in the future. Only in this way can the pitfalls of rigidity and the waste that unsuitable facilities implies be minimized.

In these final pages I have tried to select some of the most salient findings on neighboring patterns and to state explicitly their implications for physical planning.

"Whoever looks into his neighbor's face sees his own image," Lewis Mumford could write in describing neolithic village life of more than six thousand years ago.[1] This mirror image is broken now, and the social unity and cohesion that it reflected and encouraged belongs to another, a lost, era. The mosaic of conflicting and cooperating forces that now bind the members of more complex aggregates into some viable entities have given rise to a different kind of unity among men and multiplied the mirrors into which they look for glimpses of their fleeting identities. No aspect of modern life has escaped this fragmentation and regrouping, and neighboring is no exception. Not only its meaning, but also its forms and contexts of expression have changed, and this calls for changed planning concepts designed to accommodate them.

Neighbor, neighboring, and neighborhood are three distinct concepts referring to a complex set of activities and relationships within a given, variously defined, physical space. In any given settlement or population the three must be investigated independently, for while a knowledge of any one of them may throw light on the workings of the others, they are not interchangeable.

THE NEIGHBOR ROLE ■

There is no single, universally accepted definition of neighbor. Each existing definition, moreover, has both essential and variable, collective and personal, aspects. The role of neighbor does not stand alone. It is part of a network of social roles competing for the energies and time resources of individuals and reinforcing or challenging the demands and rewards of other social roles. In turn, individuals develop a set of priorities in allotting time and energies to neighbors, depending upon the strength of the collective definition and their personal needs. Other, often competing, categories of persons to which individuals relate are relatives, friends, and strangers. Despite many variations, the essential significance of the neighbors are threefold: as helpers in times of need and as sources of sociability and information.

IMPLICATION ■

Physical planners need to know the particular conception of neighbor prevalent among the people for whom they are planning. This includes ascertaining the relative strengths of collective and personal factors in the definition, the relative stress placed on help in crisis and on sociability, and the rank occupied by neighbors in the schedule of social obligations to friends, relatives, and strangers.

NEIGHBORING ACTIVITIES AND RELATIONS ▪

On investigation one will find that neighboring activities and relations vary along at least eight separate dimensions, including priority, content, formality, intensity and extent, frequency, and locale. Rural-urban and social class traditions, and social change (in values and institutions, through time, and as a result of individual and group mobility) account for most of the variations observed.

Rural-urban traditions of neighboring. Rural and urban are not to be considered dichotomous but continuous variables. In general, one may observe one type of neighboring—the solidary, integrative type that is intertwined with many other major social activities—more prevalent in rural areas, small towns, and cohesive settlements and groups in cities. Another type—segmentalized, personalized, sociable—is found in cities and urbanized areas.

Social class traditions in neighboring. Middle class individuals, whether in rural or in urban areas, are more selective, personal, and segmentalized in their neighboring than working class people. These class tendencies may either reinforce or weaken rural-urban neighboring patterns. Middle class individuals place relatively greater stress on sociability; upper class residents, on the preservations of class codes and traditions; and working class residents, on help in crisis.

Social change. As variety, heterogeneity, and individualism become socially valued and as family organization veers toward the more egalitarian, companionate type, neighboring becomes more selective and personalized and less salient than relations with spouses and friends. Residential mobility has similar effects. Perhaps as a result of the unsettling effects of the move, two distinct phases of neighboring may be observed among those moving into new communities, suburbs, and housing estates. The first consists of the tendency to be diffuse, indiscriminate, uncritical, and rather intense in one's neighboring relationships with others, especially where all settlers are newcomers. However, this diffuse sociability later gives way to the second phase—that of a more selective sociability.

IMPLICATIONS ▪

1. In general people divide their time between relatives, friends, and neighbors in varying ways in different types of settlements. Such information should guide planners in designing clubs, community centers, and transportation stops.

2. Social class and status differences affect nearly all the dimensions of neighboring because they affect the nature and definitions of crises, the availability of alternative resources, ambitions, mobility, and the time available for neighboring. Planners cannot satisfy the needs of different status groups by means of the same designs in a single neighborhood.

3. In more rural, cohesive, communal type settlements neighboring is interrelated with work, family, and leisure time pursuits and is part of a more rigidly defined collective framework. This makes the identifica-

tion of predominant conceptions and types of neighboring relatively easy. Moreover, because of the intertwining of the various components of day-to-day life with neighboring, knowing something about neighboring enables planners to know something about the other aspects of life. This is not the case in the more heterogeneous urban areas where neighboring is segmentalized, less bound by collective rules, and more diversified. There, planners must be prepared to deal with a number of conceptions of neighboring coexisting in the same physical space—the highly solidary, the anomic, and the selective variety—and they must also find ways to assess the significance of varying proportions for the overall plan.

4. Person-to-person neighboring is more prevalent and significant in the less solidary, urban areas than in the solidary, rural ones. This seeming paradox may be understood by considering the meaning of neighboring in the two settings. In the rural areas it is built around the notion of crisis and occurs within a network of relations forming part of a closed system. In the urban areas it emphasizes sociability rather than crisis and is part of a fluid, open system of shifting values and fashions. Therefore, greater attention must be paid to the tastes and habits of potential neighbors in the more urbanized areas, particularly in those economically wealthier, than in the areas of solidary neighboring whether in city or village. In the latter who lives next door matters less because reliance is placed on a whole category of people with whom one shares a particular destiny. In the former the particular individuals matter because one is interested not so much in obtaining help as in achieving emotional and personal compatibility. Planners should

thus pay greater attention to the smaller space in the larger, more diversified area.

5. The crucial determinant of neighboring in different geographical, cultural, and social class milieus seems to be the degree of self-sufficiency and autonomy. Where this is great, neighboring becomes more personal, selective, and sociable. Where it is slight, neighboring becomes more crisis-oriented and impersonal, yet solidary. Although some neighboring probably exists in all settings, the planner must expect an increase in selective, segmentalized, personal neighboring as people and areas become more heterogeneous, mobile, and urbanized for reasons of increasing self-sufficiency, individualism, and mobility.

6. A knowledge of the history of past mobility of individuals and groups helps in the assessment of their current attitudes toward neighbors. As a rule, the intense phase of sociability following a move to a new town or suburb is followed by a more settled, selective variety. Ignoring this may lead us to elevate a temporary pattern into a permanent characteristic. In thus misjudging the degree of sociability one may underestimate the needs for privacy, for example. Special formal machinery may have to be designed during the initial phase to help channel the diffuse propensity for neighboring and facilitate the integration of newcomers in a new setting.

THE NEIGHBORHOOD ■

Local areas that have physical boundaries, social networks, concentrated use of area facilities, and special emotional and symbolic connotations for their inhabitants are considered neighborhoods. The four dimensions do not overlap predictably or significantly in changing urban areas, hence the difficulty of locating neighborhoods and of planning and building effective ones. In changing urban areas, especially, the boundaries of neighbors with whom active relations are maintained do not coincide with historical, official, or physical boundaries of neighborhoods, nor with use of local facilities, nor with attachment to the local setting.

IMPLICATIONS ▪

1. Planners must keep in mind that, in general, people do not have clear-cut images of entire neighborhoods but tend to visualize only certain parts of them.

2. People draw very narrow, and often not very explicit, personal boundaries of their "neighborhoods." These boundaries may involve no more than a few houses or parts of a street, and rarely more than a few blocks. Status divisions may cut across and sharply divide the most compact street.

3. Neighboring activities and relations are highly variable in their range and characteristics in urban areas, where they tend to be informal, personally defined, selective, and subordinate to relations with immediate relatives and intimate friends. In the absence of binding collective definitions and consensus, attitudes to neighboring in urban areas will vary. Some individuals will be involved with many neighbors, others with few or none, some superficially, others intimately and extensively. The boundaries resulting from these different patterns are also highly variable, as well as small and unreliable. Strictly speaking, they are not in fact boundaries since they do not demarcate inclusive relationships but only

one among several social relationships maintained by residents.

4. The use of local facilities and services varies according to the economic, cultural, ecological, and psychological resources of the residents. No local area can today be self-sufficient in facilities and services since by that very fact it would no longer be a local area but a complex community. Therefore, no resident can rely exclusively on local resources to satisfy all the needs generated in an urban milieu. Some do so more than others, however, depending on the degree of voluntary or involuntary isolation and segregation. Planners must know the type of group for which they are designing facilities and services.

5. Different facilities tap different proportions of local users. Grocery shops located close to one's residence appear to be the one facility most frequently used and desired; but, even here, no more than 50 percent of any urban population has been found to rely exclusively on local grocery shops. Other facilities—restaurants, cinemas, parks—show similarly varied patterns of usage.

6. Objectively adequate facilities may not prevent people from moving out of an area for reasons of status, job opportunities, or merely for the sake of change and variety. The more interchangeable neighborhood facilities become, the more likely such moves will be.

7. It seems unlikely that the provision of adequate local facilities per se will increase attachment to a local area among people not otherwise favorably predisposed to it for reasons of status, personal disposition, youthful ambition, or particular value preferences.

SOCIABLE AND RESERVED NEIGHBORS ■

Studies of unplanned and planned local areas have shown that there are at least two types of individual inhabitants. Each type has different, and perhaps incompatible, conceptions of privacy, space needs, and relations to immediate and more distant neighbors. An apt description of these types refers to the one type as "sociable," to the other as "reserved." [2] The sociable resident moves into an area expecting to have warm, friendly relations with neighbors; the reserved type has no such desire. His need for privacy is stronger than his need for sociability, and the reserved resident primarily wants neighbors to respect this need. This does not, however, mean that the reserved type refuses all social contacts. On the contrary, once he is assured of the neighbors' respect for his privacy, a firm relationship, based on personal compatibility and ranging from casual politeness to intimate exchanges, may well develop with his neighbors. The crucial point is that the relationship established by reserved residents does not depend on their positions as neighbors but on their compatibility as persons, whereas for the sociable type of resident the relationship is initiated and later maintained because of the spatial position of the partners.[3]

IMPLICATIONS ■

Kuper has shown that if the reserved and the sociable types are placed side by side, both are likely to be dissatisfied since they make incompatible demands upon each other. The reserved type tends to withdraw and resents the sociable overtures of others as intrusions; the sociable type resents the other's indifference and rejection and feels lonely and ill at ease. These two types do not readily mix. The reserved type needs privacy and to be selective and more formal in his relations; the sociable type is informal and seeks to extend neighbor relations beyond neighborly bounds. Their spatial arrangements should be adapted to these deep-seated preferences.

LOCAL- VERSUS URBAN-ORIENTED INDIVIDUALS ■

A related distinction contrasts a local with an urban orientation to life. The locally oriented resident concentrates on the immediate local area for the satisfaction of basic needs—social, personal, and material—whereas the urban-oriented type uses local facilities, services, and contacts in a much more limited and less exclusive way, essentially looking to the wider society for these things. The local type resides in the city but lives in the neighborhood; the urban type resides in the neighborhood but lives in the city.

IMPLICATIONS ■

If planners could distinguish the local from the urban type and plan different facilities for each, they might find their efforts amply rewarded. The local type wants or needs to depend on neighbors and thus wants facilities nearby. The urban type, however, while not unsociable, seeks amusement and gratifications away from the local scene. How these two types relate to the differentiation between reserved and sociable is not yet clear, but the reserved type may be more urban, the sociable type, more local.

RESPECTABLE AND ROUGH RESIDENTS ■

Another typology reflects the status distinctions made by residents. A common one is that between the "respectable" and the "rough" [4] that may subdivide otherwise quite homogeneous groups and classes. The specific characteristics of these types varies by culture and setting, but the differentiation itself is made within as well as between social classes. The rough elements are considered morally inferior by the respectable, and these, in turn, are considered snobbish by the rest.

IMPLICATIONS ■

The meaning of the distinction between rough and respectable residents must be carefully understood by planners since the two mix badly if at all.[5] The respectable are home-centered, conventional, usually better off financially, and morally more consistent and controlled. The rough are often relatively poor, more disorganized, and unconventional in manners and morals, especially when seen from the perspective of middle class morality or through the eyes of the respectable residents. There may be some overlap between respectable and reserved and rough and sociable residents.

Rather than mix rough and respectable residents, perhaps only respectable residents but from adjacent status or class levels might be placed in the same area. This would help attain some of the variety desired and at the same time avoid some of the more common difficulties characterizing "mixed" neighborhoods in planned, new communities.

GROUPS WITH SPECIAL TIES ■

There are, of course, the groups with special ties to the local area—the aged, the ill, the recent migrants, the young housewives with young children, and the poor. Some of these would seem to be particularly dependent on the environment immediately adjacent to their own dwellings, including next door neighbors; others may use the facilities and services of a wider but still local area. Some of these individuals and groups because of their extreme dependence on immediate surroundings may be less critical and selective regarding neighbors and neighborhood facilities. If they cannot afford to be highly discriminating, they may be more willing to accept ethnic and status differences in order to satisfy other more important needs for help during emergencies or for human contacts to avoid loneliness. Then there are those individuals whose unstable personal lives, often reinforced by low income or poor management of available financial resources, often find themselves in critical situations where they need the help or solace of neighbors. All of these groups, incidentally, may become less dependent on neighbors once they acquire telephones or cars. These permit them to draw on more distant relatives, friends, or public services.

IMPLICATIONS ■

There are many ways of "mixing" residents in a relatively confined area. In addition to the question of who is being placed side by side, there is also that of how, and this is where the physical planner's key stock in trade enters full force. By various siting and design mechanisms planners can increase or decrease physical and functional distance and thereby promote or reduce "passive" contacts among residents. It is not true, as a number of studies have shown, that a decrease in physical and functional distance automatically helps to promote friendly social contacts, if not friendships, among the residents. In some cases reduced physical distance increases hostility and friction among neighbors because of more fundamental differences in their orientations and ambitions. Under certain special social conditions, however, decreasing physical and functional distance may result in more and friendlier social contacts among residents, although even here physical factors do not play an autonomous role.

CONCLUSION ■

This review has tried to show that the problem of neighbor relations and activities in local urban areas is complex and many-sided, and the best design on paper may turn to naught if some of the more salient social determinants of neighboring and neighborhoods are ignored. Of the two, it is easier to study neighboring than neighborhoods because neighboring takes place everywhere to some extent.

No fool-proof method for locating neighborhoods exists as yet for the simple reason that there are ever fewer fool-proof neighborhoods—neighborhoods that are self-contained, distinctive, and relatively stable. Where such neighborhoods do exist, any and all the criteria used to find them (boundaries, residents' feelings, concentrated use of neighborhood facilities, and extensive neighbor relations) are valid and useful indicators.

Where they do not exist, these criteria are of no great help. It would, perhaps, be possible to develop criteria tapping neighborhood potential in a given area, but this has not been done.

Another problem confronting physical planners and their collaborators is the absence of objective or agreed-upon standards of evaluation of functioning neighborhoods. How can we relate people's attitudes to objective facilities if we do not know how to evaluate these facilities and thus have no clear idea as to what people's attitudes should be? This question is important quite apart from the fact that to ask the right questions is itself an art that planners may do well to cultivate.

One implication of the methodological considerations discussed in this study is that once physical planners become convinced of the utility of sociological information, they must try to formulate their needs for data rather precisely. Only in this way is a fruitful collaboration between social scientists and planners likely to be established. There are no shortcuts to obtaining such data, but one necessary step may well be to restudy and reassess already existing information buried in journals that planners may not read and that social scientists may not use. In my own view, such a reexamination of existing evidence, illustrated by this study as but one instance, is a prelude to the comprehensive, carefully designed new investigations that will help us make better plans in the future.

Notes

INTRODUCTION

1. One of the chief critics is Reginald Isaacs, "The Neighborhood Theory," *Journal of the American Institute of Planners*, 14 (Spring 1948), 15–23. See also, Judith Tannenbaum, "The Neighborhood: A Socio-Psychological Analysis," *Land Economics*, 24 (November 1948), 358–69.

2. Svend Riemer, "Villagers in Metropolis," *British Journal of Sociology*, II, 1 (March 1951), 31–43.

3. Catherine Bauer, *Social Questions in Housing and Town Planning* (London: University of London Press, 1952), p. 26.

4. C. A. Doxiadis, "The Ancient Greek City and the City of the Present," *Ekistics*, 18, 108 (November 1964), 360.

5. Bauer, *op. cit.*, p. 26.

6. Doxiadis, *op. cit.*, p. 360.

7. Charles Horton Cooley, *Social Organization* (New York: Schocken, 1962), pp. 23–31.

8. Svend Riemer, "Hidden Dimensions of Neighborhood Planning," *Land Economics*, 26 (May 1950), 197.

9. Mary W. Herman, *Comparative Studies of Identification Areas in Philadelphia*, City of Philadelphia Community Re-

newal Program, Technical Report No. 9, April 1964, (mimeographed).

10. Theodore Caplow, Sheldon Stryker, and Samuel E. Wallace, *The Urban Ambience* (Totowa, N.J.: Bedminster, 1964), The Interview Schedule.

CHAPTER 1

1. Peter Townsend, *The Family Life of Old People* (Baltimore: Penguin, 1963), Chap. 10.
2. *Ibid.*, pp. 139, 140.
3. *Ibid.*, p. 145.
4. Elizabeth Bott, *Family and Social Network* (London: Tavistock, 1957), p. 67.
5. *Neighborhood and Community* (Liverpool: Liverpool University Press, 1954), p. 70. See also Leopold Rosenmayr (ed.), *Wohnen in Wien* (Vienna: Stadtbauamt der Stadt Wien. 1956), p. 59; John Gulick, Charles E. Bowerman, and Kurt W. Back, "Newcomer Enculturation in the City: Attitudes and Participation," in F. Stuart Chapin, Jr., and Shirley F. Weiss (eds.), *Urban Growth Dynamics in a Regional Cluster of Cities* (New York: Wiley, 1962), p. 339; Rainer Mackensen, J. C. Papalekas, E. Pfeid, W. Schuette, and L. Burckhardt, *Daseinsformen der Grossstadt* (Tuebingen: Mohr, 1959), Chap. 4.
6. H. E. Bracey, *Neighbors, Subdivision Life in England and the United States* (Baton Rouge: Louisiana State University Press, 1964), Chap. 5. See also Leo Kuper (ed.), *Living in Towns* (London: Crescent, 1953), p. 43.
7. Thus Fava used Wallin's neighboring scale in studying the propensity for neighboring among socially similar, ecologically dissimilar, samples of residents, and Caplow and his co-workers applied a scale of neighboring intensity in their San Juan study. See Sylvia Fleiss Fava, "Contrasts in Neighboring: New York City and a Suburban Community," in William M. Dobriner (ed.), *The Suburban Community* (New York: Putnam, 1958), pp. 123–31; Theodore Caplow, Sheldon Stryker, and Samuel E. Wallace, *The Urban Ambience* (Totowa, N. J.: Bedminster, 1964).

Bott proposes tracing through networks of social relationships in urban areas rather than sampling proportions only. See Bott, *op. cit.*, p. 49.

8. Mackensen *et al.*, *op. cit.*; Gulick *et al.*, *op. cit.*, p. 340. See also Norman Dennis, "Who Needs Neighbors?" *New Society*, 43 (July 25, 1963), 8.

9. Bracey, *op. cit.*, Chap. 5.

10. Mackensen *et al.*, *op. cit.*

11. J. M. Mogey, *Family and Neighborhood; Two Studies in Oxford* (London: Oxford University Press, 1956), p. 95.

12. Gerhard Wurzbacher, *Das Dorf im Spannungsfeld Industrieller Entwicklung* (Stuttgart: Ferdinand Encke, 1961), pp. 132 ff.

13. Mackensen *et al.*, *op. cit.*

14. Daniel M. Wilner, R. P. Walkley, T. C. Pinckerton, and M. Tayback, *The Housing Environment and Family Life* (Baltimore: Johns Hopkins Press, 1962), p. 165.

15. The concept of "latent" neighborliness is Peter H. Mann's. See his "The Concept of Neighborliness," *American Journal of Sociology*, LX, 2 (September 1954), 164.

16. Wurzbacher, *op. cit.*, pp. 112–41. In the past the poor people of the village would try to save oil and petrol at night by spending their evenings in the houses of some more fortunate neighbors. Also, in these villages, local personalities, such as traders, artisans, and especially innkeepers, would become foci for meetings and principal sources of information. *Ibid.*, p. 123.

17. Michael Young and Peter Wilmott, *Family and Kinship in East London* (New York: The Free Press, 1957). See also Herbert J. Gans, *The Urban Villagers* (New York: The Free Press, 1962).

18. *Neighborhood and Community*, *op. cit.*, p. 108.

19. Charles Vereker and J. B. Mays, *Urban Redevelopment and Social Change* (Liverpool: Liverpool University Press, 1961), p. 79. See also Mogey, *op. cit.*, p. 96.

20. Wurzbacher, *op. cit.*, Chap. 5.

21. R. P. Dore, *City Life in Japan* (Los Angeles: University of California Press, 1958), p. 257.

22. Mogey documents the increased reliance on friends as sources of help and social contact for two British working class hous-

ing estates. On the new estate 70 percent of the workers had friends, whereas on the older traditional estate only 40 per cent did. Mogey, *op. cit.*, p. 59.

23. Mackensen *et al.*, *op. cit.*, Chap. IV.

24. Ministry of Housing and Local Government, *Grouped Flat- lets for Old People: A Sociological Study* (London: Her Ma- jesty's Stationery Office, 1962), p. 21.

25. Mackensen *et al.*, *op. cit.*; Mogey, *op. cit.*, p. 83.

26. Wurzbacher, *op. cit.*, Chap. 5.

27. Mackensen *et al.*, *op. cit.*, p. 167.

28. *Ibid.*

29. Dore, *op. cit.*, p. 255.

30. One-half of the elderly residents of a group of flatlets in England visited a neighbor every day and four-fifths once a week. Ministry of Housing and Local Government, *op. cit.*, p. 33.
    In a low income sample of Baltimore housewives, from one-half to three-fourths either visited or were visited by neighbors once a week. Wilner *et al.*, *op. cit.*, pp. 161 ff.

31. Mackensen *et al.*, *op. cit.*

32. Mogey, *op. cit.*, p. 86.

33. Eugene Litwak, "Geographic Mobility and Extended Family Cohesion," in Bartlett H. Stoodley (ed.), *Society and Self: A Reader in Social Psychology* (New York: The Free Press, 1962), p. 427.

34. Caplow *et al.*, *op. cit.*, p. 183.

35. As quoted in Stanley Alderson, *Britain in the Sixties: Hous- ing* (Baltimore: Penguin, 1962), p. 55.

36. Martin Meyersohn, "Utopian Traditions and the Planning of Cities," in L. Rodwin (ed.), *The Future Metropolis* (New York: Braziller, 1961).

37. J. H. Nicholson, *New Communities in Britain* (London: National Council of Social Service, 1961), p. 242.

38. Dore, *op. cit.*, p. 267.

39. See, among others, Young and Wilmott, *op. cit.*; Herbert J. Gans, *The Settlement House and the Attack on Urban Poverty*, paper presented at the Northeastern Regional Con- ference, Philadelphia, May 2, 1963; Mary W. Herman, *Comparative Studies of Identification Areas in Philadelphia*,

City of Philadelphia Community Renewal Program, Technical Report No. 9, April 1964 (mimeographed); Hilda Jennings, *Societies in the Making* (London: Routledge & Kegan Paul, 1962).

40. F. Zweig quoted in Alderson, *op. cit.*, p. 58.

41. Caplow *et al.*, *op. cit.*, p. 224.

42. Harold L. Wattell, "Levittown: A Suburban Community," in William M. Dobriner (ed.), *The Suburban Community* (New York: Putnam, 1958), pp. 298–99.

43. Jennings, *op. cit.*, p. 212.

44. Bott, *op. cit.*, p. 112.

45. Roger Wilson, *Difficult Housing Estates*, Pamphlet No. 5 (London: Tavistock, 1963), p. 10.

46. Bott, *op. cit.*, p. 103.

47. Paul Henri Chombart de Lauwe, *Des Hommes et des Villes* (Paris: Payot, 1965), p. 16. This author notes the existence of what might be called natural or spontaneous neighborhood units in workers' milieus, consisting of a few thousand workers who, in addition to certain cultural similarities, focus on specific shops, cafes, cinemas, churches, or schools according to a particular rhythm of collective life. The author also stresses the differences between working and middle class quarters in this regard, the middle class quarters being much less cohesive.

48. Wilson, *op. cit.*, p. 11.

49. Ministry of Housing and Local Government, *op. cit.*

50. Dennis, *op. cit.*, p. 10.

51. Wurzbacher, *op. cit.*, p. 133.

52. Mogey, *op. cit.*, p. 126.

53. Bott, *op. cit.*, p. 105.

54. Nicholson, *op. cit.*, p. 32; Wilner, *op. cit.*, p. 220.

55. J. M. Mogey, "Changes in Family Life Experienced by English Workers Moving from Slums to Housing Estates," *Marriage and Family Living*, XVII, 2 (May 1955), 125.

56. Jennings, *op. cit.*, p. 110.

57. Wilson, *op. cit.*, p. 7.

58. Nicholson, *op. cit.*, pp. 69, 70.

59. Gans, *op. cit.*

60. Bracey, *op. cit.*, pp. 72–73.

61. Nicholson, *op. cit.*, p. 32; Mogey, *Family and Neighbor-hood, op. cit.*, p. 127.

62. Nicholson, *op. cit.*, p. 14.

63. Jennings, *op. cit.*, p. 222.

64. Dore, *op. cit.*, p. 267.

65. Wilson, *op. cit.*, p. 10.

66. Mogey, *Family and Neighborhood, op. cit.*, p. 87; Jennings, *op. cit.*, p. 130; A. Schorr, *Slums and Social Insecurity* (Washington, D.C.: U.S. Department of Health, Educa-tion and Welfare, 1963), p. 26.

67. Fava, *op. cit.*, p. 127. See also W. L. Martin, "The Struc-turing of Social Relationships Engendered by Suburban Residence," in William M. Dobriner (ed.), *The Suburban Community* (New York: Putnam, 1958), p. 104. Accord-ing to David Riesman, "The non-neighborly seldom seek the suburbs," in William M. Dobriner (ed.), *The Suburban Community* (New York: Putnam, 1958), p. 386.

68. E. R. Mowrer, "The Family in Suburbia," in William M. Dobriner (ed.), *The Suburban Community* (New York: Putnam, 1958), pp. 159, 161.

69. Margaret Willis, "Designing for Privacy," *Ekistics*, 17, 98 (January, 1964), 47–51.

70. Mogey, *Family and Neighborhood, op. cit.*, p. 86.

71. Nicholson, *op. cit.*, pp. 79–80, 169.

72. *Neighborhood and Community, op. cit.*, pp. 58–61; Macken-sen *et al., op. cit.*, p. 176.

73. Bracey, *op. cit.*; Wurzbacher, *op. cit.* For contrary evidence see Mackensen *et al., op. cit.*, p. 177, where the presence of children seemed not to affect neighboring.

74. Dore, *op. cit.*; Bott, *op. cit.*, p. 69.

75. Wurzbacher, *op. cit.*, p. 122.

76. Caplow *et al., op. cit.*

77. *Ibid.*

78. R. K. Merton, "Patterns of Influence: Local and Cosmo-politan Influentials," in R. K. Merton, *Social Theory and Social Structure* (New York: The Free Press, 1957), pp. 387–420; Donald L. Foley, *Neighbors or Urbanites* (Roches-ter, N.Y.: University of Rochester, 1952).

79. W. M. Dobriner, "Local and Cosmopolitan as Contempo-

rary Suburban Character Types," in William M. Dobriner (ed.), *The Suburban Community* (New York: Putnam, 1958), pp. 132–43.

80. Kuper, *op. cit.*, p. 85.

81. *Ibid.*; L. Festinger, S. Schachter, and K. Back, *Social Pressures in Informal Groups* (London: Tavistock, 1950), p. 160.

82. J. M. Beshers, *Urban Social Structure* (New York: The Free Press, 1962), pp. 118–21; H. M. Hodges, Jr., *Social Stratification* (Cambridge, Mass.: Schenkman, 1964), p. 125.

83. E. Digby Baltzell, *Philadelphia Gentlemen* (New York: The Free Press, 1958), p. 174.

84. Kuper, *op. cit.*, p. 88.

85. *Ibid.*, p. 156.

86. *Ibid.*, p. 166.

87. *Ibid.* Many other accounts confirm this.

88. Caplow *et al.*, *op. cit.*, p. 168.

89. Kuper, *op. cit.*; Wurzbacher, *op. cit.*

90. Riesman, *op. cit.*, p. 382.

91. Herman, *op. cit.*

92. Martin, *op. cit.*, pp. 95–109.

93. Herbert J. Gans, "Planning and Social Life," *Journal of the American Institute of Planners*, XXVII (May 2, 1961), 136–37.

94. Festinger *et al.*, *op. cit.*, p. 157.

95. Gans, "Planning and Social Life," *op. cit.*

96. Schorr, *op. cit.*, p. 26.

97. Kuper, *op. cit.*, p. 110.

98. *Ibid.*, pp. 140, 159.

99. Schorr, *op. cit.*

00. M. Deutsch and M. E. Collins, *Interracial Housing* (Minneapolis: University of Minneapolis Press, 1951).

01. Kuper, *op. cit.*, p. 27.

02. *Neighborhood and Community*, *op. cit.*, p. 115.

03. Mogey, *Family and Neighborhood*, *op. cit.*, p. 87; Jennings, *op. cit.*, p. 130; Schorr, *op. cit.*, p. 26. Paul Ritter might conclude differently on the basis of his comparison of the effects of motor roads versus free car paths on social life

in England. The study is a very interesting one but omit a full description of the social and personal characteristic of the residents interviewed in each type of setting, which may account for the findings that the total number of con tracts is significantly greater in the path areas, from which he draws such significant inferences. For example, if w postulate that the residents in "path access" houses ar "sociable," have young children, or share certain cultural o occupational characteristics in contrast to those "reserved," heterogeneous residents occupying "motor road access houses, then the greater sociability of the former could b quite differently explained. In fact, one of his own finding suggests that this may be the case. Ritter found that "nex door neighbor only" contact was considerably greater amon the road access households than among the path acces ones. This recalls Kuper's findings of the reserved type o residents' inclination, if they neighbor at all, to relate t one or two immediate neighbors. Another remark furthe strengthens our argument. Ritter found twice as man households with children among established path acces households as among the road access households. Thu self-selection rather than the nature of the physical environ ment may account for his findings. He himself suggests tha families with children prefer path access houses, but the he cannot attribute the sole causal connection betwee sociability and site features to the site features. Paul Ritte *Planning for Man and Motor* (Long Island City, N.Y. Pergamon, 1964), pp. 27 ff.

CHAPTER 2

1. Ruth Glass (ed.), *The Social Background of a Plan* (Lon don: Routledge & Kegan Paul, 1948), p. 18.
2. Roland L. Warren, *The Community in America* (Chicago Rand McNally, 1963), p. 24.
3. Charles Vereker and J. B. Mays, *Urban Redevelopment an Social Change* (Liverpool: Liverpool University Press, 1961 p. 79.
4. Mary W. Herman, *Comparative Studies of Identificatio Areas in Philadelphia*, City of Philadelphia Community R

newal Program, Technical Report No. 9, April 1964 (mimeographed), p. 4.

5. N. Foote, J. Abu-Lughod, M. M. Foley, and L. Winnick, *Housing Choices and Housing Constraints* (New York: McGraw-Hill, 1960), p. 181.

6. For a brief overview of the Chicago School's work see E. W. Burgess and D. J. Bogue, "Research in Urban Society: A Long View," in Burgess and Bogue (eds.), *Contributions to Urban Sociology* (Chicago: University of Chicago Press, 1964), pp. 1–14.

7. Glass, *op. cit.*

8. Herman, *op. cit.*

9. Warren, *op. cit.*, pp. 24–25.

10. S. Riemer, "Villagers in Metropolis," *British Journal of Sociology*, II, 1 (March 1951), 31–43.

11. See D. D. McGough, *Social Factor Analysis, Community Renewal Program*, City of Philadelphia Community Renewal Program, Technical Report No. 11, October 1964 (mimeographed).

12. Glass, *op. cit.*

13. Herman, *op. cit.*

14. McGough, *op. cit.*

15. *Ibid.* See also W. Bell, "Social Areas: Typology of Urban Neighborhoods," in M. B. Sussman (ed.), *Community Structure and Analysis* (New York: Crowell, 1959), pp. 61–92.

16. D. E. Baltzell, *Philadelphia Gentlemen* (New York: The Free Press, 1958), pp. 182, 194.

17. Theodore Caplow, Sheldon Stryker, and Samuel E. Wallace, *The Urban Ambience* (Totowa, N.J.: Bedminster, 1964); Norman Dennis, "Who Needs Neighbors?" *New Society*, 43 (July 25, 1963).

18. See the Improvement Index in Caplow *et al.*, *op. cit.*

19. See R. L. Wilson, "Liveability of the City: Attitudes and Urban Development," in F. Stuart Chapin, Jr., and Shirley F. Weiss (eds.), *Urban Growth Dynamics in a Regional Cluster of Cities* (New York: Wiley, 1962), pp. 359–99.

20. Glass, *op. cit.*, p. 41.

21. Caplow *et al.*, *op. cit.*, p. 31.

22. Wilson, *op. cit.*, p. 380.
23. McGough, *op. cit.*, p. 19.
24. Herman, *op. cit.*, p. 2.
25. *Ibid.*, p. 6.
26. H. L. Ross, "The Local Community: A Survey Approach," *ASR*, 27, 1 (February 1962), 78.
27. P. Wilmott, "Housing Density and Housing Design," *Town Planning Review*, XXXIII, 2 (July 1962), 124.
28. See, for example, Riemer, *op. cit.*, p. 35.
29. Hilda Jennings, *Societies in the Making* (London: Routledge & Kegan Paul, 1962), p. 222.
30. *Neighborhood and Community* (Liverpool: Liverpool University Press, 1954), pp. 106–7.
31. Herman, *op. cit.*, pp. 2, 11.
32. Wilmott, *op. cit.*, p. 125.
33. Herbert J. Gans, *The Urban Villagers* (New York: The Free Press, 1962), p. 11.
34. Rainer Mackensen, J. C. Papalekas, E. Pfeid, W. Schuette and L. Burckhardt, *Daseinsformen der Grossstadt* (Tuebingen: Mohr, 1959), Chap. 4.
35. Gans, May 1963, *op. cit.*, p. 4.
36. *Neighborhood and Community*, pp. 50 ff.
37. J. M. Mogey, *Family and Neighborhood: Two Studies in Oxford* (London: Oxford University Press, 1956), p. 141.
38. Herman, *op. cit.*, p. 17; H. E. Bracey, *Neighbors, Subdivision Life in England and the United States* (Baton Rouge: Louisiana State University, 1964), p. 39; Ross, *op. cit.*
39. W. L. Warner and L. Srole, *The Social Systems of American Ethnic Groups* (New Haven: Yale University Press, 1945), p. 50.
40. Mogey, *op. cit.*, p. 153.
41. Wilmott, *op. cit.* See also *Neighborhood and Community*, pp. 92 ff.; Jennings, *op. cit.*, p. 117.
42. Herman, *op. cit.*, p. 17.
43. H. Cohen, "Social Surveys as Planning Instruments for Housing," in R. K. Merton (ed.), *Journal of Social Issues*, VII, 1 & 2 (1951), 35–46.
44. McGough, *op. cit.*, p. 54; H. L. Ross also found food shop

ping to be a local activity; church attendance, work, and entertainment, less so. Clearly nonlocal activities were shopping for clothing or furniture. Ross, *op. cit.* See also *Neighborhood and Community, op. cit.*, pp. 93, 95, 104.

45. Mogey, *op. cit.*, p. 93.
46. A. Schorr, *Slums and Social Insecurity* (Washington, D.C.: U.S. Department of Health, Education and Welfare, 1963), p. 41. See also the observation that younger age groups may use clubs near at hand but adolescents already "prefer to go farther afield." J. H. Nicholson, *New Communities in Britain* (London: National Council of Social Services, 1961), p. 137.
47. Glass, *op. cit.*, p. 41. Compare with the following observations: "There is good reason to believe that the level of functioning of local areas in cities is limited, but there is in all probability considerable variation in the sense of community and the nature and type of social functioning among different types of areas within a city." Herman, *op. cit.*, p. 14.
    Janowitz suggests the term "community of limited liability" to connote the partial and selective character of residents' orientation to local areas. See Ross, *op. cit.*
48. See Wilson, *op. cit.*, p. 370. See also Foote *et al., op. cit.*; Athens Technological Institute, *The Human Community*, R-ACE-1-20; Bracey, *op. cit.*; John Gulick, Charles E. Bowerman, and Kurt W. Back, "Newcomer Enculturation in the City: Attitudes and Participation," in F. Stuart Chapin, Jr., and Shirley F. Weiss (eds.), *Urban Growth and Dynamics in a Regional Cluster of Cities* (New York: Wiley, 1962).
49. Caplow *et al., op. cit.*, p. 199.
50. N. Glazer and D. McEntire, *Studies in Housing and Minority Groups* (Los Angeles: University of California Press, 1960), p. 163.
51. Herbert J. Gans, *The Urban Villagers* (New York: The Free Press, 1962).
52. M. Fried and P. Gleicher, "Some Sources of Residential Satisfaction in an Urban Slum," *Journal of the American Institute of Planners*, 27 (1961), 305–15.

53. Herman, *op. cit.*, p. 11.
54. W. H. Sprott, *Human Groups* (Baltimore: Penguin, 1958), p. 90. See also Leopold Rosenmayr (ed.), *Wohnen in Wien* (Vienna: Stadtbaumt der Stadt Wien, 1956), p. 61.
55. See Caplow *et al.*, *op. cit.*, p. 202; Gans, *Urban Villagers*, *op. cit.*; Foote *et al.*, *op. cit.*, p. 183.
56. Foote *et al.*, *op. cit.*, p. 183; Herman, *op. cit.*, p. 11; McGough, *op. cit.*
57. Wilson, *op. cit.*, pp. 381, 385 ff.
58. R. P. Dore, *City Life in Japan* (Los Angeles: University of California Press, 1958), pp. 11 ff.
59. *Conference on Space, Science, and Urban Life* (Washington, D.C.: National Aeronautics and Space Administration, 1963), p. 215.
60. Mogey, *op. cit.*, p. 153.
61. See Caplow *et al.*, *op. cit.*, p. 201; Foote *et al.*, *op. cit.*, p. 184. "To attract upper class residents, an area should contain, in addition to the homes they want, a church, a club, an inn, railroad connections, and have something like a horseshow." Baltzell, *op. cit.*, p. 205.

   Many writers have found property ownership to be strongly related to residential satisfaction. An exception may be found in Caplow *et al.*, *op. cit.*, p. 212.
62. Vereker and Mays, *op. cit.*, pp. 95, 108–9; Caplow *et al.*, *op. cit.*, pp. 199, 201. For an early and the most thorough analysis of residential mobility see Peter H. Rossi, *Why Families Move* (New York: The Free Press, 1955).
63. Rossi, *op. cit.*, pp. 197, 198, 214; P. Wilmott, *The Evolution of a Community* (London: Routledge & Kegan Paul, 1963); Gulick *et al.*, *op. cit.*, p. 341. Wilner *et al.*, *op. cit.*, in Chap. XIV did not find this to be the general rule.
64. F. M. Colborn, *The Neighborhood and the Urban Renewal* (New York: National Federation of Settlements and Neighborhood Centers, 1963), p. 59.
65. Foote *et al.*, *op. cit.*, pp. 204 ff.
66. "City people . . . merely *reside* in residential areas in contrast to *living* in rural or village neighborhoods as was true in the past." Reginald Isaacs, "The Neighborhood Theory,"

Journal of the American Institute of Planners, 14, 2 (Spring 1948), 18.

CHAPTER 3

1. Ebenezer Howard proposed the creation of Garden Cities consisting of 30,000 people and subdivided into wards of 5,000 people representing a cross section of the community in each. These "wards" were to have their own primary schools, local governments, and radial road boundaries. Ebenezer Howard, *Garden Cities of Tomorrow* (London: Faber and Faber, 1902).

2. James Dahir, *The Neighborhood Unit Plan, Its Spread and Acceptance* (New York: Russell Sage Foundation, 1947). The first public mention of the neighborhood unit occurred in 1923 when Clarence A. Perry, then a worker in the American Community Center movement, read a paper entitled "A Community Unit in City Planning and Development" to a joint meeting of the American Sociological Society and the National Community Center Association. The first mention in print appears in Perry's Monograph 1, "The Neighborhood Unit, A Scheme for the Family-Life Community" in Volume 7 of the *Regional Survey of New York* (New York: Regional Plan Association, 1929). See also Perry's *Housing for the Machine Age* (New York: Russell Sage Foundation, 1939), Chap. 9.

3. Sir Alker Tripp, Assistant Commissioner of the Metropolitan Police of London, in 1942 proposed the theory of precinct planning. Agreeing with Le Corbusier that road traffic conditions had rendered the all-purpose highway obsolete, he proposed a scheme of roads of arterials to form a national network, subarterials to connect this network with towns, and local roads with limited access to subarterials and no access to arterial roads. Areas served by a local system of minor roads would thus be created within which industrial, business, shopping, and residential activities could take place. Each of these areas, or "precincts," would be distinct "centers of life and activity." In a similar vein, Colin Buchanan speaks of "environmental areas." See

J. Tetlow and others, *Homes, Towns and Traffic* (New York: International Publications Service, 1965), pp. 41 ff.

4. A. Gallion, *The Urban Pattern* (Princeton: Van Nostrand, 1963), pp. 250–64; Peter H. Mann, *An Approach to Urban Sociology* (London: Routledge & Kegan Paul, 1965), pp. 17 ff; and Tetlow and others, *op. cit.*, pp. 28 ff. and Chap. 5.

5. See "Draft Report Theme 2," *Ekistics*, 18 (1964), 283–88.

6. Gallion, *op. cit.*, pp. 250–64.

7. A. Goss, "Neighborhood Units in British New Towns," *Town Planning Review*, XXXII, 1 (April 1961), 66–82.

8. S. Khan, *Social Needs in Neighborhood Planning*, thesis presented to the Graduate School of Ekistics of the Athens Technological Institute, June 1961, p. 119. This study provides interesting information on the types of facilities desired close to home by a low income group from a non-Western culture. For example, the institution of purdah and the religious customs of the people made it desirable to have mosques much closer to their residences, thus serving a smaller number than originally envisaged. In addition, since local prejudices were not in accord with national educational aspirations and policies, the planned-for school for girls was barely used and thus superfluous.

9. See, for example, L. R. Vagale, "Neighborhood Planning and Its Relation to Housing," the summary of a lecture at Bangalore, June 19, 1964, for an in-service training course organized by the National Buildings Organization, New Delhi. This summary contains observations regarding the application of the neighborhood unit in India. See also, Paul Ritter, *Planning for Man and Motor* (Long Island City, N. Y.: Pergamon, 1964), p. 115. Ritter feels that neighborhood units have not been properly designed.

10. In the British New Towns, for example, even "the neighbourhood unit with 10,000 population proved unsatisfactory because units as large as this tend to be polycentered. Where low densities are adopted, they also tend to be unsatisfactory in size—neither small enough for a sufficiently intimate community nor large enough for a district of a town." Tetlow and others, *op. cit.*, p. 111.

11. "Draft Report Theme No. 2," *op. cit.*

12. Goss, *op. cit.*, p. 82.

13. See Ritter, *op. cit.*, p. 115.

14. Nicholson, *op. cit.*, p. 76.

15. Rainer Mackensen, J. C. Papalekas, E. Pfeid, W. Schuette, and L. Burckhardt, *Daseinformen der Grossstadt* (Tuebingen: Mohr, 1959), p. 163.

16. Elizabeth Bott, *Family and Social Network* (London: Tavistock, 1957), pp. 99, 103. See also the reference to Sweetser's "relational-personal" areas as one of five possible types of urban neighborhoods. Richard Dewey, "The Neighborhood, Urban Ecology and City Planners," in Paul K. Hatt and Albert J. Reiss, Jr. (eds.), *Cities and Society* (New York: The Free Press, 1957), pp. 783–90.

17. One of the earliest proponents of a twofold unit was Henry S. Churchill, *The City Is the People* (New York: Reynal and Hitchcock, 1945). See also J. Tyrrwhitt, "Town Planning at the Local Level," *The Municipal Journal* (February 10, 1950). Similarly, a recent United Nations Symposium acknowledged the existence of interest relationships that transcend spatial boundaries by recommending that planners think in terms of a small, local, housing neighborhood and a larger (45,000 people), more fully equipped residential sector. "Draft Report Theme No. 2," *op. cit.*

18. Leo Kuper (ed.), *Living in Towns* (London: Crescent, 1953), p. 131.

19. *Ibid.*, pp. 168–69.

20. Mann, *op. cit.*, p. 171.

21. Nicholson, *op. cit.*, p. 41; Arthur Glikson, "Urban Design and New Towns and Neighborhoods," *Landscape Architecture* (April 1962), p. 171.

22. Mann, *op. cit.*, p. 154.

23. Hilda Jennings, *Societies in the Making* (London: Routledge & Kegan Paul, 1962), p. 225.

24. Tetlow and others, *op. cit.*, p. 124. Another variation of the neighborhood unit idea is that of neighborhood cluster as it operates in Harlow, with four neighborhood units designed to serve 3,000 to 4,000 persons around three major subcenters serving 17,000 to 25,000 people. This makes

possible better quality and more variety in goods and services. *Ibid.*, p. 114.

25. S. Riemer, "Hidden Dimensions of Neighborhood Planning," *Land Economics*, 26 (May 1950), 197–201.

26. *Ibid.*, p. 197.

27. *Ibid.*

28. Paul Henri Chombart de Lauwe, *Des Hommes et des Villes* (Paris: Payot, 1965), p. 16.

29. For a discussion of the MARS plan, see Arthur Korn, *And History Builds the Town* (New York: British Book Center, 1953), pp. 83–103. For the hierarchy of communities proposed by Doxiadis see his numerous writings as well as reports in *Ekistics*.

30. Jennings, *op. cit.*, p. 225.

31. The pattern for Chicago was duplicated in twenty-two other American cities, leading the authors to conclude that "the distribution of juvenile delinquents in space and time follows the pattern of the physical structure and of the social disorganization of the American city." E. W. Burgess and Donald J. Bogue, "The Delinquency Research of Clifford R. Shaw and Henry D. McKay and Associates," in Burgess and Bogue (eds.), *Contributions to Urban Sociology* (Chicago: University of Chicago Press, 1963), p. 607.

32. *Ibid.*, p. 608.

33. Jane Jacobs, *The Death and Life of Great American Cities* (New York: Random House, 1961), pp. 112–40. For other illustrations of community action programs see M. Millspaugh and G. Breckenfeld, *The Human Side of Urban Renewal* (New York: Ives and Washburn, 1960), pp. 227–33, and Severyn T. Bruyn, *Communities in Action* (New Haven: College and University Press, 1963).

CHAPTER 4

1. Lewis Mumford, *The City in History* (New York: Harcourt, Brace & World, 1961), p. 18.

2. Leo Kuper (ed.), *Living in Towns* (London: Crescent, 1953).

3. *Ibid.*, pp. 163–64. See also Jessie Bernard, "An Instrument for the Measurement of Neighborhoods with Experimental

Applications," *Southwestern Social Science Quarterly* (September 1937), pp. 145–58.

4. Kuper, *op. cit.*

5. For more elaborate discussion, see S. Keller, "Social Class in Physical Planning," *International Social Science Journal*, XVIII, 4 (1966), 494–512.

Bibliography

Aalto, Alvar. "Feinde der Architektur." *Schöner Wohnen* (September 1965), p. 37.

Alderson, Stanley. *Britain in the Sixties: Housing.* Harmondsworth: Penguin, 1962.

Alexander, Christofer. "The City Is Not a Tree." Architectural Forum (April and May 1965).

Allen, Walter. "Secret City." *New Statesman,* Vol. 71 (February 26, 1965).

Alston, John C. *Cost of a Slum Area.* Wilberforce, Ohio: Wilberforce State College, 1948.

Anderson, Nels. "Diverse Perspectives of Community." *International Review of Community Development,* No. 7 (1961), pp. 15–33.

Angus, Anne. "Middle Class Cheshire." *New Society* (April 8, 1965), pp. 5–7.

Baltzell, Digby E. *Philadelphia Gentlemen.* New York: The Free Press, 1958.

Ban, John. "New Towns as Anti-Ghettoes?" *New Society,* Vol. 5, No. 131 (April 1, 1965).

Baranov, N. V. (chairman) (USSR). "Planning and Construction of New Towns." United Nations Symposium, *Ekistics,* Vol. 18, No. 108 (November 1964), pp. 283–288.

Bauer, Catherine. *Social Questions in Housing and Town Planning*. London: University of London Press, 1952.

Bell, Wendell. "Social Areas: Typology of Urban Neighborhoods," in *Community Structure and Analysis*. Marvin B. Sussman, editor. New York: Thomas Y. Crowell Co., 1959, pp. 61–92.

———. "Social Choice, Life Styles, and Suburban Residence," in *The Suburban Community*. Dobriner, editor. New York: 1958, pp. 225–247.

Bernard, Jessie. "An Instrument for the Measurement of Neighborhood with Experimental Applications." *Southwest Social Science Quarterly*, Vol. XVIII (September 1937), pp. 145–158.

Beshers, James M. *Urban Social Structure*. New York: The Free Press, 1962.

Beyer, Glenn H. "Home Selection and Home Management." *Marriage and Family Living*, Vol. XVII, No. 2 (May 1955), pp. 143–153.

———. *Housing: A Factual Analysis*. New York: Macmillan, 1958.

Bohlke, Robert H. "Social Mobility, Stratification, Inconsistency and Middle Class Delinquency." *Social Problems*, Vol. 8, No. 4 (Spring 1961), pp. 350–363.

Bott, Elizabeth. *Family and Social Network*. London: Tavistock Publications, 1957.

Bracey, H. E. *Neighbors, Subdivision Life in England and the United States*. Baton Rouge: Louisiana State University Press, 1964.

Brutn, Severyn T. *Communities in Action*. New Haven: College and University Press, 1963.

Burgess, E. W., and D. J. Bogue. "The Delinquency Research of Clifford R. Shaw and Henry D. McKay and Associates," in *Contributions to Urban Sociology*. E. W. Burgess and D. J. Bogue, editors. Chicago: University of Chicago Press, 1964, pp. 590–615.

Camus, Albert. "A Writer's Notebook." *Encounter*, Vol. XXV, No. 3 (March 1965), pp. 25–26.

Caplow, Theodore, Sheldon Stryker, and Samuel E. Wallace.

The Urban Ambience. Totowa, N. J.: Bedminster, 1964.

Chapin, F. Stuart, Jr., and Shirley F. Weiss, editors. *Urban Growth Dynamics in a Regional Cluster of Cities.* New York: Wiley, 1962. Chapter X: Newcomer Enculturation. Chapter XI: Liveability of the City.

Chombart de Lauwe, P. *The Sociology of Housing: Research Methods and Future Perspectives.* Rotterdam: Conseil International du Bâtiment, 1959, pp. 1–23.

Churchill, Henry S. *The City Is the People.* New York: Reynal and Hitchcock, 1945.

Cohen, Henry. "Social Surveys as Planning Instruments for Housing." *Journal of Social Issues,* Vol. VII, Nos. 1 & 2 (1951), pp. 35–46.

Cohen, Lillian. "Los Angeles Rooming House Kaleidoscope." *American Sociological Review,* Vol. 16, No. 3 (June 1951), pp. 316–326.

Colborn, Fern M. *The Neighborhood and Urban Renewal.* New York: National Federation of Settlements and Neighborhood Centers, 1963.

Cunningham, James V. *The Resurgent Neighborhood.* Notre Dame, Indiana: Fides Publishers, 1965.

"DA Projects Revisited—Eastwick, Philadelphia." *DA Review* (October 1, 1965), p. 11.

Dahir, James. *The Neighborhood Unit Plan, Its Spread and Acceptance: A Selected Bibliography with Interpretative Comments.* New York: Russell Sage Foundation, 1947.

Dean, John P. "The Ghosts of Home Ownership." *Journal of Social Issues* (1951), pp. 59–68.

Dennis, Norman. "Who needs Neighbors?" *New Society,* Vol. 3, No. 43 (July 25, 1963).

Deschamps, Fanny. "Parisiennes Décentralisées." *Elle* (1965).

Deutsch, Karl W. "On Social Communication and the Metropolis," in *The Future Metropolis.* Lloyd Rodwin, editor. New York: Braziller, 1961, pp. 129–143.

Deutsch, Morton, and M. E. Collins. *Interracial Housing.* Minneapolis: Minneapolis University Press, 1951.

Dewey, Richard. "The Neighborhood, Urban Ecology and City Planners," in *Cities and Societies.* Paul K. Hatt and

Albert J. Reiss, Jr., editors. New York: The Free Press,
1957, pp. 783–790.

———. "The Rural-Urban Continuum: Real But Relatively Un-
important." *American Journal of Sociology*, Vol. LXVI,
No. 1 (July 1960), pp. 60–66.

Dobriner, William M., editor. *The Suburban Community*. New
York: G. P. Putnam's Sons, 1958.

———. "Local and Cosmopolitan as Contemporary Suburban
Character Types," in *The Suburban Community*. William
M. Dobriner, editor. New York: G. P. Putnam's Sons,
1958, pp. 132–143.

Dore, R. P. *City Life in Japan*. Los Angeles: University of California Press, 1958.

Doxiadis, C. A. "The Ancient Greek City and the City of the
Present." *Ekistics*, Vol. 18, No. 108 (November 1964)
(reprint).

———. "The Image of the City." *DA Review*, Vol. 1, No. 9
(September 1, 1965), pp. 12–16.

Duhl, Leonard J., editor. *The Urban Condition*. New York:
Basic Books, 1963.

Dyckman, John. "The Changing Uses of the City," in *The
Future Metropolis*. Lloyd Rodwin, editor. New York:
Braziller, 1961.

Fava Fleis, Sylvia. "Contrasts in Neighboring: New York City
and a Suburban Community," in *The Suburban Community*. William M. Dobriner, editor. New York: G. P.
Putnam's Sons, 1958, pp. 123–131.

Feldman, Arnold S., and Charles Tilly. "The Interaction of
Social and Physical Space." *American Sociological Review*, Vol. 25, No. 6 (December 1960), pp. 877–884.

Fellin, Phillip, and Eugene Litwak. "Neighborhood Cohesion
Under Conditions of Mobility." *American Sociological
Review*, Vol. 28, No. 3 (June 1963), pp. 364–377.

Festinger, Leon, Stanley Schachter, and Kurt Back. *Social Pressures in Informal Groups. A Study of Human Factors
in Housing*. London: Tavistock Publications, 1950.

Foley, Donald L. *Neighbors or Urbanites*. Rochester: University
of Rochester, 1952.

———. "The Use of Local Facilities in a Metropolis," in *Cities and Societies*. P. K. Hatt and A. J. Reiss, Jr., editors. New York: The Free Press, 1959, pp. 607–616.

Foote, Nelson N., Janet Abu-Lughod, Mary Mix Foley, and Louis Winnick. *Housing Choices and Housing Constraints*. New York: McGraw-Hill, 1960.

Fried, Marc, and Peggy Gleicher. "Some Sources of Residential Satisfaction in an Urban Slum." *Journal of American Institute of Planners*, Vol. XXVII (1961), pp. 305–315.

Galamison, Milton A. "Bedford-Stuyvesant—Land of Superlatives." *Freedomways*, Vol. 3, No. 3 (Summer 1963).

Gans, Herbert J. "The Balanced Community." *Journal of American Institute of Planners*, Vol. XXVII, No. 3 (August 1961), pp. 176–184.

———. *Effects of the Move from City to Suburb.*

———. "Park Forest: Birth of a Jewish Community." *Commentary*, Vol. II (April 1951), pp. 330–339.

———. "Planning and Social Life." *Journal of American Institute of Planners*, Vol. XXVII (May 2, 1961), pp. 134–140.

———. "The Settlement House and the Attack on Urban Poverty." Prepared for presentation at the 1963 Northeastern Regional Conference, Philadelphia (May 2, 1963).

———. "The Suburban Community and Its Way of Life: Notes Toward a Description and an Evaluation." Paper read at the Eastern Canadian Sociological Association Conference, Toronto (February 15, 1963).

———. *The Urban Villagers*. New York: The Free Press, 1962.

Glass, Ruth, editor. *The Social Background of a Plan: A Study of Middlesborough*. London: Routledge & Kegan Paul, 1948.

Glazer, Nathan. "The Problem of Poverty and Race." *Ekistics*, Vol. 18, No. 104 (July 1964), pp. 25–27.

Glazer, Nathan, and Davis McEntire. *Studies in Housing and Minority Groups*. Los Angeles: University of California Press, 1960.

Glikson, Artur. "Urban Design and New Towns and Neighborhoods." *Landscape Architecture*, Vol. 52 (April 1962), pp. 169–172.

Goss, Anthony. "Neighborhood Units in British New Towns."

The Town Planning Review, Vol. XXXII, No. 1 (April 1961), pp. 66–82.

Gross, Llewellyn. "The Use of Class Concepts in Sociological Research." *American Journal of Sociology,* Vol. LIV, No. 5 (March 1949), pp. 409–421.

Gulick, John, Charles E. Bowerman, and Kurt W. Back. "Newcomer Enculturation in the City: Attitudes and Participation," in *Urban Growth Dynamics in a Regional Cluster of Cities,* Stuart F. Chapin and Shirley F. Weiss, editors. New York: Wiley, pp. 315–358.

Gutkind, E. A. *Revolution of Environment.* London: Routledge & Kegan Paul, 1946.

Hartman, Chesher W. "Social Values and Housing Orientations." *Ekistics,* Vol. 17, No. 98 (January 1964), pp. 52–56.

Henry, Jules. "White People's Time, Colored People's Time." *Transactions,* Vol. 2, No. 3 (March-April 1965), pp. 31–34.

Herman, Mary W. *Comparative Studies of Identification Areas in Philadelphia.* City of Philadelphia Community Renewal Program, Technical Report No. 9, April 1964 (mimeographed).

Hodges, Harold M., Jr. *Social Stratification.* Cambridge, Mass.: Schenkman, 1964.

Howard, Ebenezer. *Garden Cities of Tomorrow.* London: Faber and Faber, 1902.

Hyman, Sidney. "Washington's Negro Elite." *Look* (April 6, 1965).

Issacs, Reginald. "The Neighborhood Theory." *Journal of the American Institute of Planners,* Vol. XIV, No. 2 (Spring 1948), pp. 15–23.

Jackson, J. B. "Cumbernauld." *Landscape,* Vol. 12, No. 3 (Spring 1963), pp. 17–19.

Jacobs, Jane. *The Death and Life of Great American Cities.* New York: Random House, 1961.

Jennings, Hilda. *Societies in the Making.* London: Routledge & Kegan Paul, 1962.

Kahn, J. H. "A Psychiatrist on New Towns." *Town and Country Planning* (October 1961).

Khan, S. *Social Needs in Neighborhood Planning.* Thesis presented to the Graduate School of Ekistics, Athens Technological Institute, in partial fulfillment of the M.A. degree (June 1961).

Keller, Suzanne. "The Role of Social Class in Physical Planning." *International Social Science Bulletin,* Vol. XVIII, No. 4 (1966).

Koppe, William A. "The Psychological Meanings of Housing and Furnishings." *Marriage and Family Living,* Vol. XVII, No. 2 (May 1955), pp. 129–132.

Korn, Arthur. *And History Builds the Town.* New York: British Book Center, 1953.

Kuper, Leo, editor. "Blueprint for Living Together," in *Living in Towns,* Kuper, ed. London: Cresset, 1953, pp. 1–203.

Lee, Rose Hum. "The Decline of China Towns in the U.S." *American Journal of Sociology,* Vol. LIV, No. 5 (March 1949), pp. 422–432.

Litwak, Eugene. "Geographic Mobility and Extended Family Cohesion," in *Society and Self.* Bartlett H. Stoodley, ed. New York: The Free Press, 1962, pp. 416–430.

McGee, T. G. "The Cultural Role of Cities: A Case Study of Kuala Lumpur." *Ekistics,* Vol. 18, No. 104 (July 1964), pp. 19–22.

McGough, Donna M. *Social Factor Analysis.* City of Philadelphia Community Renewal Program, Technical Report No. 11, October 1964 (mimeographed).

McGovern, P. D. "New Towns as Regional Centers." *Town and Country Planning,* Vol. XXIX, No. 6.

Mackensen, Rainer, J. C. Papalekas, E. Pfeid, W. Schütte, and L. Burckhardt. *Daseinsformen der Grossstadt.* Tuebingen: J. C. B. Mohr, 1959, pp. 158–225.

Mackenzie, Norman. "Epitaph for a Borough." *New Statesman,* Vol. 71 (April 2, 1965).

McKinley, Donald Gilbert. *Social Class and Family Life.* New York: The Free Press, 1964.

Madge, Janet H. "Some Aspects of Social Mixing in Worcester," in *Living in Towns.* Leo Kuper, editor. London: Cresset, 1953, pp. 267–294.

Mann, Peter H. An Approach to Urban Sociology. London: Routledge & Kegan Paul, 1965.

————. "The Concept of Neighborliness." American Journal of Sociology, Vol. LX, No. 2 (September 1954), pp. 163–168.

Martin, Walter J. "The Structuring of Social Relationships Engendered by Suburban Residence," in The Suburban Community. William M. Dobriner, editor. New York: G. P. Putnam's Sons, 1958, pp. 95–108.

Mays, John B. "New Hope in New Town." New Society, Vol. 3, No. 47 (August 22, 1963).

"Mental Health Aspects of Urbanization." Report of a Panel Discussion, World Federation for Mental Health (March 11, 1957).

Merton, Robert K. "Patterns of Influence: Local and Cosmopolitan Influentials," in Social Theory and Social Structure. Robert K. Merton, editor. New York: The Free Press, 1957, pp. 387–421.

Mestechkin, S. "Planning in the Kibbutz." Landscape Architecture (April 1962), pp. 173–175.

Meyersohn, Martin. "Utopian Traditions and the Planning of Cities," in The Future Metropolis. Lloyd Rodwin, editor. New York: Braziller, 1961.

Meyerson, Martin. "What Specific Implications does Expanding Technology have upon the Problem of Metropolitan Areas?" in Seminar E, Conference on Space, Science and Urban Life, Washington, D.C.: National Aeronautics and Space Administration, 1963.

Millspaugh, Martin, and Gurney Breckenfeld. The Human Side of Urban Renewal. New York: Ives and Washburn, 1960.

Ministry of Housing and Local Government. Grouped Flatlets for Old People: A Sociological Study. London: Her Majesty's Stationery Office, 1962.

Mitchell, G. Duncan, et al. Neighbourhood and Community. Liverpool: Liverpool University Press, 1954.

Mogey, J. M. "Changes in Family Life Experienced by English Workers Moving from Slums to Housing Estates." Marriage and Family Living, Vol. XVII, No. 2 (May 1955), pp. 123–132.

————. *Family and Neighborhood: Two Studies in Oxford.* London: Oxford University Press, 1956.

Mowrer, Ernest R. "The Family in Suburbia," in *The Suburban Community.* William M. Dobriner, editor. New York: G. P. Putnam's Sons, 1958, pp. 147–164.

————. "The Isometric Map as a Technique of Social Research." *American Journal of Sociology,* Vol. XLIV, No. 1 (July 1938), pp. 86–97.

Mumford, Lewis. "The Neighborhood and the Neighborhood Unit." *Town Planning Review,* Vol. XXIV, No. 4 (January 1954), pp. 256–270.

Nicholson, J. H. *New Communities in Britain.* London: N.C.S.S., 1961.

Norton, Perry L. "A Note on 'Community'," in *Planning and the Urban Community.* Harvey Perloff, editor. Pittsburgh: University of Pittsburgh Press, 1961.

Osborn, Frederic J., and Arnold Whittick. *The New Towns, the Answer to Megalopolis.* London: Leonard Hill, 1963.

Perry, Clarence Arthur. "The Neighborhood Unit." *Regional Survey of New York and Its Environs,* VII. New York: Committee on Regional Plan of New York and Its Environs, 1929, pp. 22–140.

Pittman, David J. "Homeless Men." *Transactions,* Vol. 1, No. 2 (January 1964), pp. 15–16.

Porterfield, Austin L. "Traffic Facilities, Suicide, and Homicide." *American Sociological Review,* Vol. 25, No. 6 (December 1960), pp. 897–901.

"The Psychological Dimension of Architectural Space." *Progressive Architecture* (April 1965), pp. 159–167 (editorial feature).

Reiner, Thomas A. *The Place of the Ideal Community in Urban Planning.* Philadelphia: University of Philadelphia Press, 1963.

Reiss, Albert J., Jr., and Albert Lewis Rhodes. "The Distribution of Juvenile Delinquency in the Social Class Structure." *American Sociological Review,* Vol. 26, No. 5 (October 1961), pp. 720–732.

Remy, Jean. *Charleroi et son Agglomération.* Brussels: Centre de Recherches Socio-religieuses et SODEGEC, 1964.

Riemer, Svend. "Hidden Dimensions of Neighborhood Planning." *Land Economics*, Vol. 26, No. 2 (May 1950), pp. 197–201.

———. *The Modern City*. Engelwood Cliffs, N.J.: Prentice-Hall, 1952.

———. "Villagers in Metropolis." *British Journal of Sociology*, Vol. II, No. 1 (March 1951), pp. 31–43.

Riesman, David. "The Suburban Sadness," in *The Suburban Community*. William M. Dobriner, editor. New York: G. P. Putnam's Sons, 1958, pp. 375–402.

Ritter, Paul. *Planning for Man and Motor*. New York: Macmillan, 1964.

Rodwin, Lloyd, editor. *The Future Metropolis*. New York: Braziller, 1961.

Rogler, Lloyd H. "A Better Life: Notes from Puerto Rico." *Transactions*, Vol. 2, No. 3 (March-April 1965), pp. 34–36.

Rosenmayr, Leopold. "Wohnverhältnisse und Nachbarschaftsbeziehungen," in *Wohnen in Wien*. Leopold Rosenmayr, editor. Vienna: Stadtbauamt der Stadt Wien, 1956, pp. 37–91.

Rosow, Irving. "The Social Effects of the Physical Environment." *Journal of American Institute of Planners*, Vol. XXVII, No. 2 (May 1961), pp. 127–134.

Ross, H. Laurence. "The Local Community: A Survey Approach." *American Sociological Review*, Vol. 27, No. 1 (February 1962), pp. 75–84.

Rossi, Peter. *Why Families Move*. New York: The Free Press, 1955.

Schnore, Leo F. "Some Correlates of Urban Size: A Replication." *American Journal of Sociology*, Vol. LXIX, No. 2 (September 1963), pp. 185–193.

Schorr, A. *Slums and Social Insecurity*. Washington, D.C.: U. S. Department of Health, Education and Welfare, Social Security Administration, 1963.

Schroeder, Clarence W. "Mental Disorders in Cities." *American Journal of Sociology*, Vol. XLVIII, No. 1 (July 1942), pp. 40–47.

Slater, Philip E. "On Social Regression." *American Sociological Review*, Vol. 28, No. 3 (June 1963), pp. 339–363.

Sorokin, Pitrim. *Social and Cultural Mobility.* New York: The Free Press, 1959.

Spencer, John. *Stress and Release in an Urban Housing Estate.* London: Tavistock Publications, 1964.

Sprott, W. H. *Human Groups.* Baltimore: Penguin, 1958.

Stinchcombe, Arthur L. "Institutions of Privacy in the Determination of Police Administrative Practice." *American Journal of Sociology,* Vol. LXIX, No. 2 (September 1963), pp. 150–160.

Strotzka, Hans. "Spannungen und Lösungsversuche in Städtischer Umgebung," in *Wohnen in Wien.* Leopold Rosenmayr, editor. Vienna: Stadtbauamt der Stadt Wien, 1956, pp. 95–108.

Sussman, Marvin B., editor. *Community Structure and Analysis.* New York: Thomas Y. Crowell, 1959.

Tetlow, John, and Anthony Goss. *Homes, Towns and Traffic.* London: Faber and Faber, 1965.

Tyrwhitt, Jaqueline. "The Size and Spacing of Urban Communities." *Journal of American Institute of Planners,* Vol. XV, No. 3 (Summer 1949), pp. 10–17.

———. "Town Planning at the Local Level." *The Municipal Journal* (February 10, 1950).

Vagale, L. R. "Neighbourhood Planning and Its Relation to Housing." Summary of Lecture at Bangalore, June 19, 1964, in Service Training Course organized by the National Buildings Organization, New Delhi.

Vereker, Charles and J. B. Mays. *Urban Redevelopment and Social Change.* Liverpool: Liverpool University Press, 1961.

Vernon, Raymond. *The Myth and Reality of Our Urban Problems.* Cambridge, Mass.: Joint Center for Urban Studies of the Massachusetts Institute of Technology and Harvard University, 1962.

Vogt, Evon Z., and Thomas F. O'Dea. "A Comparative Study of the Role of Values in Social Action in Two Southwestern Communities." *American Sociological Review,* Vol. 18 (1953), pp. 645–654.

Warner, Lloyd W., and Paul S. Lunt. *The Social Life of a Modern Community.* New Haven: Yale University Press, 1941.

Warner, Lloyd W., and Leo Srole. *The Social Systems of American Ethnic Groups.* New Haven: Yale University Press, 1945.

Warren, Roland L. *The Community in America.* Chicago: Rand McNally, 1963.

Wattel, Harold L. "Levittown: A Suburban Community," in *The Suburban Community.* William M. Dobriner, editor. New York: G. P. Putnam's Sons, 1958, pp. 287-313.

Whyte, William H., Jr. *The Organization Man.* London: Jonathan Cape, 1957.

Willems, Emilio. "Racial Attitudes in Brazil." *American Journal of Sociology,* Vol. LIV, No. 5 (March 1949), pp. 402-408.

Willis, Margaret. "Designing for Privacy." *Ekistics,* Vol. 17, No. 98 (January 1964), pp. 47-51.

Wilmott, Peter. *The Evolution of a Community: A Study of Dagenham After Forty Years.* London: Routledge & Kegan Paul, 1963.

————. "Housing Density and Town Design in a New Town: A Pilot Study at Stevenage." *The Town Planning Review,* Vol. XXXIII, No. 2 (July 1962), pp. 115-127.

Wilner, Daniel M., and Rosabelle P. Walkley. "The Effects of Housing on Health, Social Adjustment and School Performance." Paper presented at the 39th Annual Meeting of the American Orthopsychiatric Association, Los Angeles (March 23, 1962).

Wilner, Daniel M., Rosabelle P. Walkley, Thomas C. Pinckerton, and Matthew Tayback. *The Housing Environment and Family Life.* Baltimore: Johns Hopkins Press, 1962.

Wilson, Robert L. "Liveability of the City: Attitudes and Urban Development," in *Urban Growth Dynamics in a Regional Cluster of Cities.* Stuart F. Chapin and Shirley F. Weiss, editors. New York: Wiley, 1962, pp. 359-399.

Wilson, Roger. "Difficult Housing Estates." Tavistock Pamphlet No. 5 (1963).

Wurzbacher, Gerhard. *Das Dorf im Spannungsfeld Industrieller Entwicklung.* Stuttgart: Ferdinand Encke, 1961, pp. 112-151.

Young, Michael, and Peter Wilmott. *Family and Kinship in East London.* New York: The Free Press, 1957.

Index

STUDIES IN SOCIOLOGY